digital™ GROWTH THROUGH TEAMWORK

CANADIAN DISTRIBUTION CONFERENCE
LE CHANTECLER SKI RESORT
STE. ADELE QUEBEC
FEBRUARY 1990

ANCIENT
CANADA

Robert McGhee

ANCIENT CANADA

illustrations
Gilles Archambault

photographs
Harry Foster

CANADIAN MUSEUM OF CIVILIZATION

series editor
André Bastien

supervisory editor
Claude Paulette

production
Henri Rivard

editorial committee
Jean-François Blanchette
Dominique Clift

text editors
Catherine Cunningham-Huston
Gene Bodzin

design
France Lafond

cover photograph
Harry Foster

typesetting and page make-up
Deval-Studiolitho

photoengraving
Adcolitho

printing
Imprimerie Boulanger

binding
Coopérative Harpell

Gilles Archambault used Strathmore Bristol Plate paper and Talens brand watercolours for his illustrations.

Illustration Credits
Except for the illustrations on the pages listed below, the drawings and watercolours are by Gilles Archambault, and the photographs are by Harry Foster, staff photographer, Canadian Museum of Civilization.

Archaeological Survey of Alberta (drawings by James D. Keyser): 107, 108-109, 110
Canadian Museum of Civilization: 16, 22, 25 (Jacques Cinq-Mars), 32 *bottom*, 33, 60, 67, 80, 81 *bottom*, 82, 90 *right*, 91 *left and right*, 93, 102, 102-103, 103, 111, 124, 129, 152, 153
Norman Clermont, Claude Chapdelaine and Georges Barré, *Le site iroquoien de Lanoraie* (Recherches amérindiennes au Québec, 1983): 143
McCord Museum, Montreal: 90 *left*
Robert McGhee: 49
Mia and Klaus: 31, 45, 87, 130, 131
François Morneau: 17
Museum of the American Indian, New York: 79
National Archives of Canada, Ottawa: 13, 72-73, 77, 81 *top*, 92, 120, 156
Ontario Ministry of Natural Resources: 78, 89
Émile Petitot, *Les Grands Esquimaux*, (Paris, 1887): 161
Royal Ontario Museum, Toronto: 32 *top*, 35

Cover photograph:
Found eroding from a sea beach in the High Arctic, this life-size mask was probably used by a Palaeo-Eskimo shaman in ceremonies to help hunters or cure the sick. Carved from driftwood and painted with red ochre, the mask was originally decorated with fur eyebrows and moustache; thin lines suggest a tattooing pattern across the forehead and cheeks and below the chin.

©Canadian Museum of Civilization, 1989
Legal deposit: 3rd quarter 1989
ISBN 0-660-10795-3

Canadian Cataloguing in Publication Data

McGhee, Robert, 1941-

Ancient Canada

Issued also in French under title: Le Canada au temps des envahisseurs.
Issued jointly with: Libre Expression.
Includes index.

ISBN 0-660-10795-3

1. Canada, Northern – History. 2 Arctic regions – Discovery and exploration. 3. America – Discovery and exploration – Pre-Columbian 4. Canada, Northern – Antiquities. 5. Inuit – Canada – Antiquities. I. Canadian Museum of Civilization. II. Title.

FC3961.M33 1989   971.9'01   C89-096292-8
F1060.7.M33 1989

Cet ouvrage a été publié simultanément en français sous le titre *Le Canada au temps des envahisseurs*.
ISBN 2-89111-371-3

CONTENTS

FOREWORD

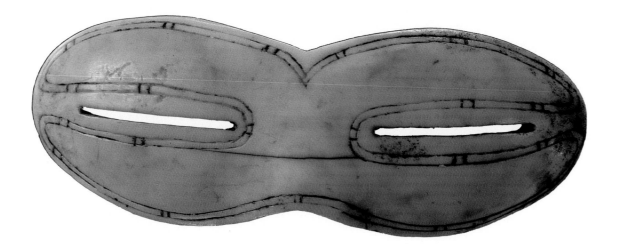

When the subject of archaeology comes up, most people think first of Greece, Egypt or Africa. Canada is usually considered too young a country to have accumulated archaeological treasures. Yet the soils of Canada hold wonderful secrets — the story of unique human adventures of which we are the fortunate heirs.

Archaeology is our guide on a journey into Canada's ancient past, a past that reveals itself only in scattered fragments. Yet these remnants gradually come together to form an image: of a land that has changed remarkably over time, and of men and women who used their intelligence and ingenuity to build remarkable ways of life adapted to their changing environments.

The Canadian Museum of Civilization is pleased to offer readers an opportunity to make this adventurous journey to ancient Canada, a journey fifteen thousand years or more into the past. To comprehend the ancient land in which we live, to meet and get to know our predecessors, allows us to gain a better appreciation for the land we live in today.

George F. MacDonald
Director
Canadian Museum of Civilization

INTRODUCTION

*"We the Original Peoples of this land know
the Creator put us here. The Creator gave us
laws that govern all our relationships to live in
harmony with nature and mankind. . . . The
Creator gave us our spiritual beliefs, our
languages, our culture, and a place on Mother
Earth which provided us with all our needs. We
have maintained our freedom, our languages,
and our traditions from time immemorial."*

From *A Declaration of the First Nations*
Assembly of First Nations, Ottawa

Canadians see themselves as a nation of immigrants. Most of us trace our ancestry from the people who left France during the seventeenth and eighteenth centuries, or the British Isles during the eighteenth and nineteenth centuries, to settle much of eastern Canada. Others are descended from nineteenth-century Asiatic immigrants to the West Coast, or from the eastern Europeans who flocked to the Prairies around the beginning of the present century. Many contemporary Canadians arrived from western Europe after the Second World War, or more recently from southern and eastern Asia, Latin America or the Caribbean. Only the Arctic Inuit can trace a local ancestry measured in thousands of years, and only the Indians can claim descent from forebears who lived here as long ago as the last ice age.

Few Canadians retain more than family ties with the "old country", and many have only family names and legends to remind them that their ancestors came from elsewhere. Consequently, many feel the occasional wistful regret that their heritage is not more deeply rooted in this country. We look at the Irish or the Greeks or the Japanese, and envy them the security and cultural richness that they seem to derive from living in their own ancestral lands and according to their own ancient traditions. This longing for a heritage no doubt explains the popularity of books suggesting early occupation of North America by Nordic, Celtic, Mediterranean, or other Old World peoples.

Yet, from an archaeological perspective, Canada is no more a nation of immigrants than is any other nation on earth. The Irish and the Greeks are descended from people who came from western Asia within the past few thousand years.

The Japanese are relatively recent immigrants from the Asian mainland, supplanting an older race now surviving only on the far northern islands of Japan. Only southern and eastern Africa, and perhaps southern Asia, can claim to be the birthplace of humanity, and even these regions are now occupied by immigrant peoples who have no closer relationship to our early human ancestors than do the rest of us.

The ability to move into new areas, even new environmental zones, and to claim them is a distinctive human characteristic. After a few generations of habitation, the descendants of the early Irish, Greeks and Japanese were able to think of themselves as having always lived in those countries: the land was theirs, and their claim was validated by myth and legend even though they may have displaced some forgotten earlier inhabitants. If non-native Canadians lack a sense of long tradition, it is because our ancestors immigrated to North America after the development of written history, which records the fact that they came from elsewhere.

Over the last one hundred years the new science of archaeology has developed methods of investigating the past by studying the remains of past activities. These methods of investigation are particularly useful in studying prehistory, that vast range of human life and experience which occurred before the development of written history. Archaeologists generally divide the past into two major periods: the "Historic period", for which contemporary written accounts are available, and the "Prehistoric period", prior to the existence of written records. In Canada the Historic period began with the arrival of Europeans and the introduction of the written word.

Archaeological reconstruction of the past is based on an objective, standardized set of procedures for recovering and interpreting information. The great advantage of this approach is that knowledge of the prehistoric past is no longer known only through the legends of individual groups. Rather, the knowledge gained through archaeology adds to the heritage of all groups, and is accessible to everyone who wishes to learn from and appreciate it.

From the archaeological perspective, all human groups have an equally long history: a record of gradually developing abilities and achievements, and a record of repeated movements and adaptations to new territories. The historical heritage of particular groups is not exclusive to them, but is part of the common heritage of humanity. It is entirely understandable that the Canadian Indians, for example, have a greater interest in their own history than in Irish or Greek or Japanese history, the Irish more interest in Irish history, and so on. Yet each group can appreciate the heritage of the others.

Archaeology, depending as it does upon material evidence of past events occurring at specific places, tends to view history as bound to a territory rather than to the groups occupying that territory today. From archaeological study emerges a history of the local landscape and environment, and an appreciation of the fact that the view from one's window today would have been very different in the distant past. Scenes could have included, at various times, a sheet of advancing ice a kilometre high, a deep arm of the sea in which whales spouted among icebergs, a tundra landscape with wandering herds of caribou and mammoths followed by Stone Age hunters recently arrived from Asia, a ceremonial procession of a later people with religious ideas and concepts of the world based on those of the pyramid builders of Mexico, and the first of the Europeans who were to transform our continent. From this perspective, the historical heritage of Canada or of specific regions of Canada belongs to and can be appreciated by all Canadians, regardless of ancestry.

This book presents the reader with a set of ancient landscapes, peoples and events, all of which have been reconstructed on the basis of archaeological excavations. The places discussed range from the coast of Labrador to the northern Yukon, and from Vancouver Island to the islands of the Arctic Archipelago; the time spanned is perhaps 20 000 years. These particular reconstructions have been chosen partly on the basis of the personal interests and experiences of the author, but also to illustrate the breadth and depth of our historical heritage. Although lacking archaeological treasures as monumental as those of Egypt, Mexico or China, Canada has a fascinating past in which we can all take pride. We owe a great deal to the native peoples, whose ancestors explored, settled and built prehistoric Canada.

CHAPTER 1

IN THE BEGINNING

During interglacial periods, ancestral humans who had learned to survive the cold, glacial conditions of mid-latitude Europe and Asia were lured northwards by the herds of animals that fed on lands freed recently from beneath the continental glaciers. Following these herds, the Stone Age hunters of eastern Siberia wandered unwittingly onto a new continent: North America.

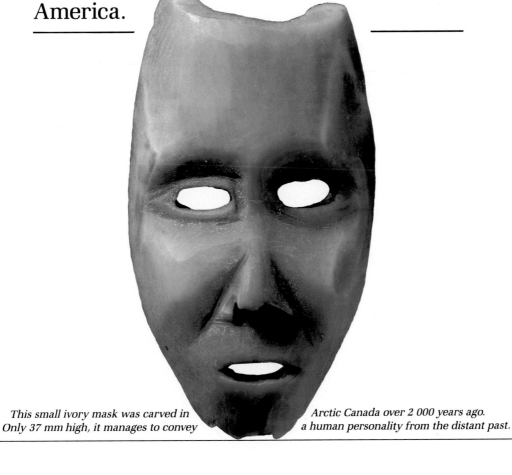

This small ivory mask was carved in Arctic Canada over 2 000 years ago. Only 37 mm high, it manages to convey a human personality from the distant past.

The human species did not evolve in Canada or in any other part of the New World. Our closest biological relatives in the Western Hemisphere are the monkeys of Central and South America, and that relationship is very distant indeed.

Over the geological ages, as animals and plants gradually developed more-complex forms, the continents were continuously moving, a massive and extremely slow wandering in which they occasionally met, causing pressures sufficient to raise folded layers of rock into mountains. Close contact between the continents of the New and the Old World last occurred tens of millions of years ago, after the extinction of the dinosaurs and at a time when the remote ancestors of humankind had evolved to a monkey-like form. In the tropical areas of the New World, these animals changed only gradually, eventually developing into the present small and long-tailed monkeys of the region. In the Old World, perhaps because it contained far larger and more-varied tropical regions, our monkey-like ancestors evolved at a more rapid rate. Some developed into the diverse species of Old World monkeys; others evolved towards the modern apes, our closest living relatives in the animal world.

An African or Asiatic Origin

Very little is known about the first creatures that could be called ancestral humans rather than ancestral apes. They probably appeared in Africa or southern Asia sometime in the past ten million years, when certain ape-like animals developed an upright two-legged posture, more-mobile hands, a larger brain, and an increasing dexterity in the use of sticks and stones to augment their physical strength. Fossil finds from Africa that are at least two or three million years old definitely appear to be ancestral to humans. Only within the past 100 000 years, however, have there existed people who, if appropriately clothed and barbered, could walk down a city street without being suspected of having escaped from a zoo.

During the past two or three million years, humans evolved toward their modern physical form and developed the languages, cultures and technologies that set them apart from other animals. This period is known to geologists as the Pleistocene – the epoch of ice ages. For almost all of this period, world climates were considerably colder than they are at present. Time and again,

The physical characteristics of native North Americans resemble those of Siberian peoples, reflecting their ancient Asiatic heritage. (See Indian boy, p. 13, and Inuit girls, p. 16.)

massive glaciers accumulated in arctic and subarctic regions, covering most of Canada, northern Europe and the mountainous regions of northern Asia with sheets of ice several kilometres thick. Environments that today are found only in arctic regions extended far southwards over the continents, while the tropics and subtropics were subjected to alternate periods of increased rainfall and desertification as weather patterns shifted from glacial to interglacial conditions.

For most of this period our ancestors remained tropical or subtropical animals. Unable to cope with the harsh climates of more-northern regions, they were as restricted to the environments to which they were biologically adapted as are the apes and bears of today. A consequence of this restriction was that, although they spread through most of the lower latitudes and eventually into the temperate regions of the Old World, they could not reach the American continents. Such an opportunity was available only to a people adapted to far-northern environments and thus capable of reaching the area where the continents of both hemispheres make their only close approach: the Bering Strait, which today separates Asia from northwestern North America by a distance of only about 100 kilometres.

Bridging Two Continents

This route to North America was available throughout most of the Pleistocene epoch. In fact, during all glacial periods, what is now the Bering Strait was a plain, up to 1 000 kilometres wide, joining Asia and North America into a single continent. The Beringian Plain was, in fact, a large area of continental shelf exposed when world sea levels dropped 100 metres or more below present levels because of the amount of water locked into continental glaciers. Only during short interglacial periods, such as the one in which we are living at present, were Asia and North America separated by a narrow strip of water. Even during the first few millennia of each interglacial period, sea levels did not rise sufficiently to totally sever the two continents.

Unlike most of Europe and northern North America, eastern Asia was virtually free of glaciation during the Ice Age. Probably because the climate was too dry to allow glaciers to accumulate,

continued page 17

Between approximately 80 000 and 20 000 years ago, almost all of Canada was buried beneath a kilometre or more of glacial ice. A large ice-free area known as the Bering Land Bridge extended from the Yukon and Alaska into Siberia. Animals and human hunters moved between the Old World and the New across this arctic landscape.

About 15 000 years ago, the glaciers began to melt and retreat. An ice-free corridor probably opened between the glaciers over Hudson Bay and those covering the western mountains. Human groups were thus able to move southwards and occupy the American continents.

By about 12 000 years ago, the glaciers were retreating rapidly and were fringed by large lakes of glacial meltwater. The ancient beaches of these lakes reveal the remains of camps occupied by Indians who moved northwards to occupy the land that is now Canada.

Canada today

Québec Since the Ice Age

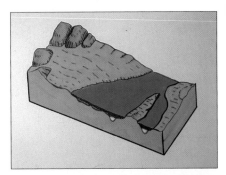

Every region of Canada was drastically changed by the events of the last ice age. The place where Québec City stands today underwent vast environmental change during and after the Ice Age. Until about 12 000 years ago, it was buried beneath hundreds of metres of glacial ice. Under the weight of this ice, the rocks on which the city now stands were pushed downwards to form a shallow depression. When the ice began to melt, the Atlantic Ocean flowed into this trough and covered the area with over 100 metres of seawater. With the weight of the ice removed, the local rocks rose and gradually emerged from the sea. The rising land forced the ocean to retreat eastwards, and the water around Québec slowly became fresher as the present course of the St. Lawrence River was established.

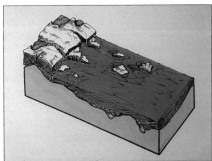

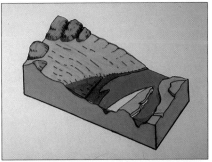

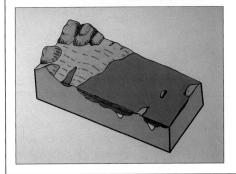

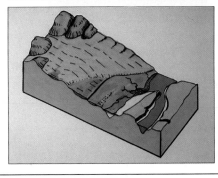

other than in mountainous regions, the cold and arid Beringian Plain extended far into Siberia to the west, and over much of Alaska and the northern Yukon to the east. Across this plain roamed most of the animals that occupy arctic regions today, as well as the many other species that became extinct at the end of the last glaciation, about 12 000 years ago – arctic-adapted species of horse, camel, bison, mammoth, and such strange animals as huge ground-sloths and giant beavers.

During each interglacial period, ancestral humans who had learned to survive the cold glacial

Inuit girls from the Central Arctic, 1915.

conditions of mid-latitude Europe and Asia must have been lured northwards by the herds of animals that fed on lands recently freed from the continental glaciers. Techniques for surviving in northern regions had gradually increased. Fire had first been controlled (a few hundred thousand years ago) by an early human creature known as *Homo erectus*. Animal skins were almost certainly worn by the Neanderthal people in the glaciated Europe and Asia of about 80 000 years ago. Before the last ice age, from about 25 000 to 12 000 B.P. (Before the present time), biologically modern *Homo sapiens* had developed efficient weapons and techniques for hunting the large herd animals of the northern plains and tundras. In Europe, these people have left us the

continued page 22

17

Routes to the New World

As European exploration advanced across and around the New World, it became apparent that the American continents were surrounded by water. Until the present century there was no reliable information on the existence of prehistoric land bridges that may have joined the New World to the Old. Nevertheless, some of the more extravagant speculation regarding the origin of the native peoples of the Americas postulated the past existence of extensive land bridges, including the mythical land of Atlantis. More commonly, however, speculation centred on possible water crossings at various times in the past, which might have either brought the ancestors of the American Indians from the Old World, or at a later date brought them the benefits of various classical Old World civilizations.

Navigational Abilities

Any consideration of such crossings must start from what we know of the boat-building and navigational abilities of ancient peoples. The earliest valid evidence of the ability of humans to cross relatively large bodies of water comes from Australia, which is now known to have been settled by the ancestors of the Aborigines no later than 30 000 years ago. To reach the subcontinent, these people had to cross at least 80 kilometres of open water, even when world sea levels were low during periods of Ice Age glaciation. Such a crossing at so early a period is very surprising and is generally considered to have occurred accidentally; perhaps a few people using a primitive raft for inshore fishing were blown out to sea and survived the few days of thirst and exposure before their craft landed on an Australian beach. Still, it suggests that our human ancestors were making use of at least primitive watercraft at a very early period.

A crossing of 80 kilometres in the relatively warm climate of Southeast Asia is, however, on a different scale from the crossing of at least 3 000 kilometres over the Atlantic or Pacific Ocean to the New World. Ships capable of such voyages were probably not developed until well into recorded history. The earliest substantial ships we know of, from rock carvings and occasional remains preserved in tombs, were Egyptian. By 2000 B.C. at the latest, the Egyptians were building large freight vessels powered by oars and square sails. Despite their size, these were essentially Nile River boats, practical for voyages along the coast but far too fragile for the open ocean. Although the Egyptians have continued to build ships for 4 000 years, they have remained a river people and never developed a craft that would have enabled them to undertake extended ocean voyages.

In the Mediterranean area this development was left to the Phoenicians of what is now Lebanon, who were building oceanworthy freighters by at least 700 B.C. According to Herodotus, a Phoenician fleet circumnavigated Africa on a three-year voyage during the sixth century B.C. Although this and all other known Phoenician voyages were made within sight of the coasts, the ships were probably capable of extensive open-water crossings. During the first century A.D., ships of similar design were used by sailors of the eastern Roman Empire to make the first known voyages across the open ocean, from the Red Sea to southern India. The voyages of Sinbad are probably not totally mythical; Arabic sailors most likely extended the navigation of the Graeco-Romans, reaching China and Japan by the ninth century A.D.

The ships of eastern Asia were developed even later than those of the West. Chinese ships ventured as far as Singapore in about A.D. 350, reached India later in the century and probably travelled as far west as the Euphrates River. Yet the Chinese, like the Egyptians, were essentially a river people, and do not seem to have been attracted to open-water voyaging. The abortive invasion of Japan made by the Emperor Kublai Khan in the thirteenth century A.D., in which the invading fleet was destroyed by a storm (the kamikaze, the "divine wind"), suggests that ancient Chinese ships were not well designed for extensive open-water crossings.

The great seafarers of southeastern Asia were not the builders of the major civilizations of China and Japan, but those who discovered and settled the vast area of Polynesia. Travelling in outrigger canoes powered by sails, navigating by the stars, the Polynesians began to spread across the Pacific between 4 000 and 3 000 years ago. By the time Euro-

The turquoise arrows show the major ocean currents that could have carried prehistoric voyagers between the Old World and the New, and the blue arrows indicate the routes that have been suggested as possible contacts between the hemispheres. Ancestral Indians almost certainly reached America from the Old World during the last ice age by way of a land bridge joining Alaska to eastern Siberia.

pean explorers reached the Pacific, the Polynesians had discovered and settled such isolated islands as Hawaii and Easter Island.

We now know that humans reached the New World more than 12 000 years ago, and that the roots of the major New World civilizations extend as far back as the first or second millennium B.C. Since Old World peoples learned to navigate the open ocean only much later, it is apparent that neither the peoples of the New World, nor elements of their culture,

reached the American continents by water. Nevertheless, occasional accidental drift voyages to the New World may have occurred, and it is worthwhile to look briefly at their possible effects.

The North Atlantic

Speculation on North Atlantic crossings focuses on Palaeolithic Europeans voyaging in skin boats along the edge of the Ice Age pack ice and becoming the ancestors of the Amerindians; Neolithic Scandinavians making a similar crossing (as

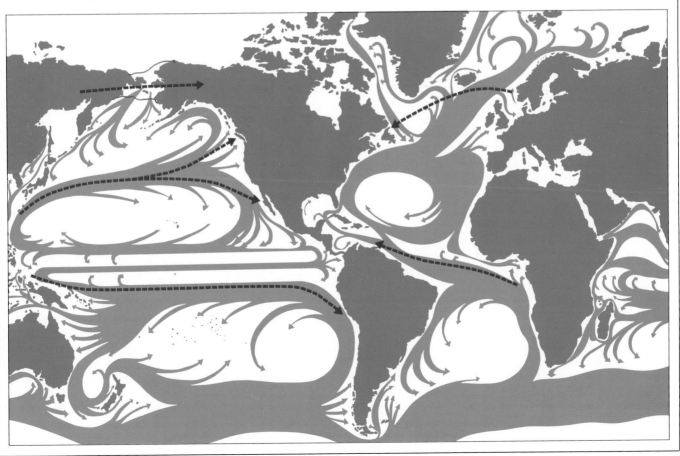

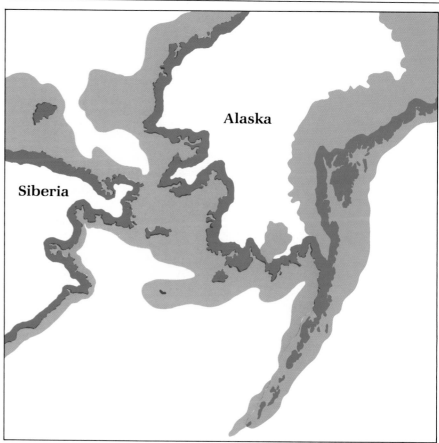

present coastlines

exposed seabed of Beringia

Ice Age glaciers

Siberia

Alaska

suggested by similarities between the ground-stone tools of northern Europe and those of eastern North America approximately 5 000 to 3 000 years ago); ancestral Eskimos crossing the pack ice from northern Russia to Greenland; and more recent expeditions by the Irish and the Norse. On a more southerly course, Egyptians and Phoenicians have been considered as possible early navigators of the Atlantic.

The North Atlantic is a notoriously stormy ocean, and any route south of Iceland and Greenland would require an open-water crossing of approximately 3 000 kilometres, against the flow of the Gulf Stream current and against the prevailing westerly winds. As we have seen, European and Mediterranean peoples probably did not have ships capable of making such a crossing until the first millennium A.D., and it is highly unlikely that any maritime contact between the New and Old worlds occurred before that time. The first European navigators who were capable of reaching North America and were interested in voyaging far to the west were probably the Irish. Travelling in large skin-covered boats similar to the Inuit umiak, Irish monks reached Iceland by the eighth century A.D., but there is no evidence that they travelled farther west. Following the Irish, the Norse discovered Greenland in the tenth century and shortly thereafter began to make at least occasional voyages to the coast of eastern Canada. Although the Norse are known to have crossed the Atlan-

tic and probably made at least one abortive attempt to settle in Canada, there is no evidence that they had more than a merely local influence on the inhabitants of the New World.

The South Atlantic

Early voyages from Africa to South America are suggested by the facts that some South American Indians are relatively dark-skinned and that some early stone tools from South America bear a resemblance to tools of the late African Stone Age. The Olmec civilization of the last millennium B.C. in Mexico produced a number of large stone carvings depicting people with apparently Negroid features. However, the dark skin colour of tropical Indians is almost certainly the result of adaptation to the high light levels of southern latitudes, as well as of interbreeding with African slaves brought to the New World over the past few centuries. The similarities between early stone tools in Africa and South America are very general, and not strong evidence of contact. The giant carved stone heads of the Olmec remain a mystery. A crossing of the South Atlantic is as long as a voyage

across the North Atlantic – approximately 3 000 kilometres – but southern crossings are aided by warm temperatures, the South Equatorial current and the trade winds. On the other hand, the canoe-type crafts developed by the Africans for river travel and coastal fishing were probably unequal to extensive ocean voyages. While such craft may occasionally have drifted to the New World, and their passengers may even have survived, the evidence for African contact is extremely slight. While accidental crossings of the South Atlantic are theoretically possible, if any occurred they almost certainly had little influence on the development of the cultures and civilizations of the New World.

The North Pacific

The North Pacific Ocean is approximately twice as wide as the Atlantic, but is crossed from west to east by prevailing westerly winds and by the North Pacific current. During the past few centuries, occasional Chinese and Japanese fishing junks have accidentally drifted across this ocean, landing on coasts from Alaska to Mexico. Such drift voyages have been cited as the basis for speculation that the roots of New World civilization were introduced from eastern Asia.

The major problem with these theories is one of timing. As we have seen, the peoples of eastern Asia did not develop major maritime abilities until 2 000 years ago. After this time, survivors of a drift voyage from the Orient would have encountered Mexican and South American civilizations in full flower. One must also question the ability of survivors, close to death from thirst and exposure, to change the course of New World history. More likely, the sailors of a Chinese or Japanese junk wrecked on the coast of Mexico would have been treated as were a sixteenth-century Spanish crew whose ship was wrecked on the coast of Yucatan. Sixteen of the eighteen crew members were sacrificed, and the other two were enslaved; six years later, when Cortés arrived, both survivors were indistinguishable from the local Indians, and one refused to leave his captors.

The South Pacific

The Polynesians seem to have been the first people on earth to develop the technology and the skills for extensive ocean voyaging. Yet their farthest settlement, Easter Island, is more than 3 000 kilometres from the coast of South America, and prevailing winds and currents must have discouraged exploration farther east. Contacts between Polynesia and the New World have been suggested, but generally involving traffic from east to west. Speculation ranges from Thor Heyerdahl's theory that the Polynesians came from South America (which led to his famed Kon-Tiki drift expedition) to theories that the Haida Indians of British Columbia introduced dugout canoes and totem poles to peoples as far away as New Zealand.

The major evidence for a west-to-east contact comes from Ecuador, where about 30 years ago archaeologists discovered a style of pottery very similar to Japanese wares of about 5 000 years ago. Although the resemblances are striking, evidence accumulated over the past decades strongly suggests that they are coincidental. Not only do the Ecuadorian and Japanese potteries now seem to date from different periods, but the pottery of Ecuador can be shown to have developed from a local industry, whose early products bore no resemblance to those of the Japanese. At a much more basic level of analysis, one must wonder how a member of a Japanese fishing crew could have survived an accidental voyage from Japan to British Columbia or California, and how he eventually reached Ecuador and became a skilled potter.

Despite the evidence against any major water-borne traffic between the Old and New worlds, occasional and accidental contacts between the two hemispheres probably did occur over the past few thousand years. A few Chinese or Japanese fishing junks, their crews barely alive, may have fetched up on the west coast of North America. A few African dugout canoes may have reached the Caribbean, and a few Polynesian outriggers may have landed on the west coast of South America. We know that the Norse reached eastern Canada; before them a boatload of Irish monks, searching for God far from the haunts of men, may have landed on the coasts of Labrador or Newfoundland.

There is no evidence that such contacts had any influence on the development of the civilizations of the New World. Most such travellers would have met a fate similar to that of the Spanish crew wrecked on the coast of Yucatan; they would either have been killed or have adopted the ways of the local people. Nor did the contacts occur in only one direction; it is likely that over the past few thousand years some Indian canoes would have been blown far from shore, eventually to reach Polynesia, Europe or Africa. Any sailors who survived apparently had no major influence on Old World civilizations. The best evidence for such contacts lies in a few European museums that contain Inuit kayaks, apparently blown to sea from Greenland and beached on the shores of Scotland and northern Germany. Farley Mowat's fictional reconstruction of the life of one such kayaker, who ended his days as a Scottish fisherman spending quiet Saturday nights in the village pub, is more plausible than any of the theories that entire civilizations were transferred between the Old and New worlds by accidental voyagers.

legacy of the painted caves, which testify to their ability to live a satisfactory life in the cold northern climate of a glacial period.

Far to the east, by the beginning of the last ice age, similar hunters of mammoth, horse, bison and reindeer had penetrated to the Arctic Circle in the region of present-day Yakutsk. During the glacial period, people spread eastwards to Kamchatka and northwards almost to the Arctic coast. The Beringian Plain was occupied by herds of animals that, never having encountered humans, must have been easy prey to hunters. Following these herds, the Stone Age hunters of eastern Siberia wandered unwittingly onto a new continent.

These first immigrants to the New World were the ancestors of the American Indians. Their descendants were to occupy two continents and, in virtual isolation from the Old World, develop ways of life and cultures parallel to those of Old World peoples. Their history, as yet poorly known, covers a span of years over 20 times as long as the history of European settlement in the Americas. Only through the accidents of archaeological preservation are we allowed occasional glimpses of the history of those first immigrants to the New World – a few isolated snapshots, torn and faded with age, showing groups of people leading ways of life very different from those of the modern world.

CHAPTER 2

THE FIRST INHABITANTS

During the closing phases of the last ice age, northwestern Canada was joined to Asia by the Beringian Plain. In the northern Yukon, excavations in a cave occupied some 15 000 to 20 000 years ago may yield evidence of the first immigrants to the New World.

Found in the Bluefish Caves, this chipped-stone tool, known as a burin, was used for carving bone or antler. It closely resembles the tools of the peoples who hunted across Europe and Asia during the last ice age.

For well over 100 000 years people have used caves as temporary shelters, as places to carry out ceremonial activities, and occasionally as permanent homes. Few, if any, of these people bore a close resemblance to the cavemen of the comic strips, and they probably thought of caves in much the same way as we do today: attractively mysterious features of the landscape, but damp and dismal places in which to live. Yet caves have always been useful refuges in times of trouble. They have provided shelter to travellers caught on a lonely hillside by nightfall or by a storm; to small communities whose valley dwellings have been inundated by spring floods; to fugitives in need of a temporary hiding place.

Caves hold a place of importance in the archaeological study of our early ancestors, not because our ancestors considered caves prime dwelling locations, but because the remains left in them had a very good chance of being preserved. During the last ice age, almost all humans lived in settlements in open country, and their tents or huts disappeared without trace soon after being abandoned. The tools, weapons and animal bones left scattered on these sites gradually disappeared too – through erosion of the site by running water, burial beneath deep deposits of drifting earth or sand, or deterioration caused by soil acids. On the few occasions that these early peoples occupied caves, however, such remains were protected from erosion and deep burial by the shelter of the cave, and from deterioration by the relatively cool cave environment.

Arctic Caves

Canada is not particularly rich in caves, and most of them are in remote areas that probably never supported dense prehistoric populations. The early Indian immigrants to Canada had developed efficient tent dwellings that were much more comfortable and convenient homes than were caves. It is very difficult to heat a cave, and in the cold Canadian climate people have always preferred homes that could be easily heated with a fire. Thus Canadian caves have generally proved disappointing to the archaeologist. Within the past few years, however, evidence of what may prove to be the oldest known archaeological site in the country has been found in a set of small caves overlooking the Bluefish River in the far-northern Yukon. Bluefish is the local name for the grayling, a beautifully iridescent fish inhabiting the rivers of northwestern North America, and the caves have become known as the Bluefish Caves.

A visit to the caves begins in the Dene Indian village of Old Crow, a community of log houses set in the spruce forest along the northern bank of the Porcupine River. From there a helicopter carries the visitor above the roofs of the village, banks over the river and heads westwards across a basin surrounded by mountains. The floor of the basin is a patchwork of spruce forest, lake and bog, divided by the muddy line of the Porcupine as it meanders westwards into Alaska to join the Yukon River. To the south, the small Bluefish River breaks out of the mountains and snakes northwards through its own flat plain. The helicopter turns to follow the Bluefish southwards, and approaches the upland areas surrounding the basin: first, low rocky ridges with sparse forest cover, then the higher hills of the Keele Range, covered with tundra vegetation and gradually rising to the Ogilvie Mountains. One of the first ridges is capped by a jagged limestone outcrop like a grey tooth rising from the green forest. As the helicopter circles the outcrop, three shallow cavities can be seen distributed around its base. The pilot lands among the sparse spruce trees on top of the outcrop, and the visitor scrambles down to inspect the caves.

Artifacts from the Old Crow River

The caves were discovered on just such a helicopter trip in 1975. Archaeologists William Irving and Jacques Cinq-Mars of the University of Toronto had recently set up camp near Old Crow to begin a long-term project investigating what appeared to be ancient artifacts exposed by the erosion of the banks of the Old Crow River. While Irving concentrated on tracking down the source of these artifacts (a source not yet found), Cinq-Mars began to search for traces of human occupation on the uplands around the Old Crow and Porcupine basins.

One day in July, Irving and Cinq-Mars decided to have a look at the country to the south of the flats and investigated this particular ridge because it looked like a prime location for an archaeological site – a hilltop from which a hunter would have an unimpeded view of the Bluefish Valley and the great stretches of the basin to the north. They landed for a quick look, taking a

Animal bones carpet the bottom of an archaeological trench extending from the mouth of the Bluefish Caves. The bones are the remains of animals that roamed the northern Yukon late in the last ice age.

shovel with them when they climbed down to the caves. The largest of the three caves turned out to be a rounded hollow dissolved out of the limestone outcrop, and measured approximately three metres across at the mouth and four metres in depth. The digging of a small hole produced only a few fragments of white caribou bone, probably the remains of a recent wolf kill, and one bone of a deep-brown colour, suggesting that it had been stained by long burial. Noting the caves for a possible future visit, they left in the hope that further exploration would produce more promising sites. They did not return until the end of the 1977 field season, when they spent a day digging an exploratory trench in the floor of the cave. Their digging produced more stained bones, but no stone tools or other recognizable signs of human activity. They again abandoned the site.

A Few Horse Bones

The archaeological potential of the Bluefish Caves was not recognized until the following winter, when a palaeontologist working with the University of Toronto team was examining the bones brought back the previous summer. She recognized that some of the bones excavated from the cave were those of horses, which had become extinct in North America around the end of the last ice age. The bones, therefore, were more than 10 000 years old, and it seemed possible that at least some of them had been carried into the cave by humans. This possibility brought Cinq-Mars back to the site for a few days in 1978. Since then he has spent four summers at the caves; his work has been sponsored by the Canadian Museum of Civilization, his current employer.

Excavation of the caves proceeded slowly and carefully, the earth scraped away with small mason's trowels and the positions of all finds recorded on a map grid. Gradually, the deposits that had accumulated over the millennia on the cave floors were revealed and deciphered. In all three caves the ground surface was underlain by a layer of humus a few centimetres thick. This layer revealed no artifacts, only a few animal bones, probably carried to the caves by carnivores. Beneath the humus was a deep layer of fine light-coloured soil interspersed with limestone rubble fallen from the roof of the caves. This layer was up to two metres thick and permanently frozen. It proved to contain a gradually accumulated record of the local climate and vegetation and the animals that lived in the area over the period of

several thousand years during which the deposit was formed.

During the last ice age, between approximately 25 000 and 12 000 years ago, ice-sheets over a kilometre thick covered most of Canada. Surprisingly, the largest areas to remain free of ice were in the Far North – the most northwesterly islands of the Arctic Archipelago, and the northern Yukon Territory. Under present conditions, these areas receive considerably less rainfall than do any other regions of the country. The situation during the Ice Age was probably similar, with insufficient snow accumulation to survive over the summer season and eventually form an ice-sheet. Glaciers did form on mountains, but these were isolated from one another by large stretches of unglaciated flats and valleys.

With ice-sheets covering the continent to the east, heavily glaciated mountains to the south and a frozen Arctic Ocean to the north, the northern Yukon was even colder and dryer than today. Yet the climate did support a tundra vegetation suitable for grazing by herbivores. These animals in turn attracted carnivores and scavengers, perhaps including Palaeolithic (Old Stone Age) hunting peoples from Asia. Both the animals and their human predators could have reached the area across the Bering Land Bridge, a tundra-covered plain over 1 000 kilometres wide; with the melting of the glaciers and the resulting rise in world sea levels, it now forms the floor of the Bering Sea.

Reconstruction of a Landscape

The nature of the Beringian Plain and its eastward extension into the northern Yukon has been reconstructed from evidence produced by archaeological, palaeontological, palaeobotanical and geological studies over the past few decades. The deposits in the Bluefish Caves fit neatly into the general picture and help to bring it into clearer focus. Sometime around 20 000 years ago, the bedrock floors of the caves began to be covered with fine wind-carried dust. This was loess, powdery "rock-flour" ground by moving glaciers, carried as silt by glacial streams and picked up as dust by the winds blowing from the ice-sheets. Until about 10 000 years ago, when the glaciers had retreated, this dust accumulated in the caves at an average rate of less than a millimetre per year. Flakes of limestone spalled by winter frost from the walls and roof of the caves piled up in the dust. The wind also introduced spores and

26

continued page 30

The Oldest Artifact in the New World?

Fashioned from the leg bone of a caribou, this was a scraper used to process the hides of animals for clothing. It was found in 1966, eroding from the bank of the Old Crow River in the northern Yukon Territory. Although it was deeply stained and was found in the same area as the bones of mammoths and other Ice Age animals that had also eroded from the riverbanks, there were no sure signs of any great age. Half of the artifact was therefore sacrificed to obtain a radiocarbon date that would reveal its actual age.

Radiocarbon dating is the most common technique for determining the age of archaeological specimens. It operates on the principle that a minute proportion of the carbon that forms the basis of most organic materials (wood, bones, teeth, etc.) is radioactive (carbon-14) and decays at a known rate to form standard non-radioactive carbon. Placing a measured sample of the ancient material in a very sensitive counting chamber and calculating the rate of radioactive decay makes it possible to estimate the material's age.

Unfortunately, in the 1960s a large amount of carbon was needed before a date could be obtained. Half of the Old Crow scraper was burned, but sufficient carbon could be obtained only by using bone apatite, an inorganic form of bone carbon that may become contaminated and yield erroneous dates. The date obtained for the scraper suggested an age of

The controversial "ancient scraper" from the Old Crow River.

27 000 years, which was consistent with the estimated age of several other bones of extinct animals from the same area. The scraper was thus widely accepted as the oldest definite artifact known from the New World.

However, this early date was not universally accepted. Most disturbing was the artifact's close resemblance to those made and used by local Dene peoples of the past few centuries; it seemed very unlikely that the style of this particular artifact had not changed in over 27 000 years.

During the 1980s a new technique of radiocarbon dating was developed, involving an atomic accelerator and direct measurement of the number of carbon-14 atoms in a sample. The advantage of this technique is that it requires a very small carbon sample; a small piece of the scraper thus contained enough organic carbon – extracted from bone protein, which is known to give more reliable readings – for a redating. In 1986, the Old Crow scraper was found to be only 1350±150 years old. Three other artifacts that had been found in similar circumstances were dated from only between 1 800 and 3 000 years ago. The similarity between these tools and those made by the ancestors of the local Dene people was therefore explained, and archaeologists became more cautious in accepting radiocarbon dates that suggested long occupation of the New World.

On the ice-age tundra of northwestern North America, dogs and man combine forces to hunt a woolly mammoth. Harassed by the dogs and impeded by the soft snow of the drift-filled ravine into which it has been driven, the largest animal of the time is incapable of escaping human hunters armed with stone-tipped spears.

pollen grains released by plants growing in the vicinity, and occasionally the leaves and other parts of plants. Birds of prey used the area as a roost, leaving behind the skeletons of the mice and voles they had eaten. Foxes, wolves and bears must have occasionally used the caves as shelters and dropped the bones of their prey in the dust of the floors.

Over a period of several millennia, these natural processes produced a deposit that can be carefully mined for information regarding the environment in which it accumulated. The animal bones can be identified to tell us what sort of creatures lived in the area and can be radiocarbon dated to assess the age of the various levels of the deposit. Pollen grains and other plant fossils provide information on local vegetation. Additional information can be gained by identifying the species of voles and mice, small animals that are adapted to very specific microenvironments; even the remains of beetles that lived in the cave tell us about the ancient environmental conditions.

Studies of this evidence show that when the Bluefish Caves began to fill with loess, the area was covered with a tundra vegetation resembling that which exists today on the islands of the Arctic Archipelago. The fauna, however, was much more diverse than that of the present Canadian Arctic. Besides the caribou, muskoxen, wolves, foxes and bears found today in arctic regions, the local Ice Age tundra was grazed by horses, bison, mountain sheep, elk and mammoths. About 14 000 years ago, there was an increase in birch pollen, indicating warmer weather and the gradual invasion of the tundra by shrubs and small trees. Finally, a rapid increase in spruce pollen marked the reforestation of the area around 10 000 years ago and brought an end to loess deposition, as vegetation covered areas that had previously been bare mud from the outwash of glaciers. It also marked the disappearance of the large tundra herbivores. For the last 10 000 years the cave deposits have accumulated very slowly, and consist mainly of the decayed remains of spruce needles and other vegetation, owl pellets, and the occasional animal bone.

An Impassable Barrier to the South

During the millennia when the continental glaciers were retreating and the Bluefish Cave

deposits were accumulating, human hunting populations were moving eastwards from Asia. They crossed the Beringian Plain into Alaska and the northern Yukon and then spread southwards to become the ancestors of the American Indians. There is great uncertainty as to when these people first reached the areas south of the ice-sheets, but the first definite and widespread occupation began about 13 000 years ago. It seems reasonable to believe that the ancestors of these people had reached the unglaciated areas of Alaska and the Yukon several millennia earlier and had been prevented from moving southwards by continental glaciers. Yet none of the northern camps of these early explorers have been found. The Bluefish Caves may be the first such site to be recognized as a place that was at least occasionally visited by ancient hunters, who left sparse evidence of their activities preserved in the deposits of the cave floors.

The best evidence of human occupation comes from the upper levels of the loess deposit, those dating between approximately 10 000 and 13 000 years ago. These levels yielded a few artifacts chipped from flint, a hard and fine-grained stone that was the major technological material of the Palaeolithic or Old Stone Age. These artifacts – a chisel-like tool called a burin, which was used for carving other tools from bone, and a knife-like tool called a microblade – are similar to tools used by Palaeolithic peoples in Siberia at about the time the Ice Age ended. Several of the animal bones recovered from these levels show nicks from a sharp flint tool. No unmistakable tools have yet been found in the lower levels of the deposit, those dating between roughly 15 000 and 20 000 years ago, but there are a few traces that suggest a human presence. These are tiny flakes of flint, probably the by-products of stone-tool manufacture; nicks on bones, suggesting that the animals had been butchered with flint knives; and a few pebbles and a large river cobble, which must have been carried to the caves from the riverbank 250 metres below. Human activity is also suggested by the large numbers of animal bones found in the loess deposits; over 10 000 bones have been recovered, representing animals as large as mammoths. None of the other caves excavated in northwestern North America have yielded such massive numbers of bones, and it seems unlikely that such an accumulation could have been left by predatory animals. One of the mammoth bones recently excavated from the lower levels of the caves had been broken by a very sharp and

30

continued page 34

A Faithful Companion

The dogs that accompanied the first Palaeo-Indians to the New World may well have resembled these dogs of today's Inuit.

The first immigrants to the New World almost certainly travelled and lived symbiotically with *Canis familiaris*, the domestic dog. Some dogs may have carried backpacks or dragged tent poles. Others may have harried mammoths during the hunt, or protected their masters' camps from the giant species of bears, wolves and cats that roamed the new country. Dogs must have spread rapidly throughout the New World with the early Palaeo-Indian hunters, and survived alongside humans to populate two continents.

An Ancient Partnership

Little is known about the ancient history of the association between humans and dogs. The fact that every society in the world lives in companionship with dogs suggests that the link is very old, almost certainly dating from the last ice age. The association of these two species probably came about accidentally, as hunters brought wolf pups to their camps as playthings. Baby animals are frequently brought home by hunting peoples today, and were likely also brought home by ancient hunters, to be discarded or eaten once they had outgrown their attractiveness as playthings. Wolf pups differ from all other baby animals, however, in that they possess a psychological bonding mechanism – not unlike that in humans – ensuring their social incorporation into the home pack. Humans and wolves also share the ability to transfer their social bonds to animals of other species. To a dog raised in a human family during the first few months of its life, the human family becomes the pack to which it owes loyalty, affection and protection. That humans are subject to similar cross-species bonding can be seen by watching dog owners in the parks of any city today.

As a result of such bonding, the phenomenon of the "one-man dog" must soon have been noted in the camps of Ice Age hunters. Captured wolf pups that formed such bonds must occasionally have survived into adulthood and have demonstrated

their usefulness to a hunting people. Indeed, the two species were very useful to each other. Living in the camps of humans, dogs received protection from their wild enemies, especially animals that might have preyed on their young. In areas where hunting was only seasonally productive, dogs were given a share of food that was stored for the seasons of scarcity; they were also fed fish, which was abundant in many regions but inaccessible to wolves or wild dogs. In return they used their acute senses of hearing and smell to warn their human companions of intruders, and if necessary would fight to the death to protect their camp. They were able to find animals hidden from a hunter and could use their superior speed and strength to run down fleeing prey, holding it or bringing it to a stand until the hunter arrived. Over the millennia they

A wool-dog sits in the foreground of this 1840s painting of a Salish house by Paul Kane.

performed other tasks: carrying and pulling, child-minding, retrieving, and constantly cleaning the camp through scavenging. Of course they also stole food, fought with other dogs, and bit people whom they considered outsiders. Their usefulness, however, must have outweighed the nuisances they caused.

Dogs or Wolves?

Archaeology has not been of much help in discovering when people and dogs began to live together. The skeletons of dog-like animals are found in archaeological sites dating from the distant past, but the bones of any large dog are almost indistin-

Dog burial in a 3 500-year-old Indian settlement in Ontario.

guishable from those of its wild brother, the wolf. Canines can be recognized in ancient carvings and cave-paintings, but it is impossible to tell whether these animals represent companions or competitors in the hunt. The earliest direct evidence of a domesticated dog comes from Ushki-1, an archaeological site on the Kamchatka Peninsula of northeastern Siberia. There, in 1972, Soviet archaeologist N.N. Dikov found a canine skeleton beneath the floor of a dwelling that was occupied sometime between 10 000 and 11 000 years ago. The animal lay on its left side with the paws curled up as if asleep; a whetstone and two tools chipped from obsidian were found beside it, and there were traces of red ochre on the skeleton. The apparent ceremony displayed in the burial is similar to that seen in human burials of the time. It leaves little doubt that this was not a wild beast, but a valued friend that would be missed by the people who buried it beneath the earth floor of their house.

In their culture and way of life, the people who lived at Ushki-1 must have been very similar to those who crossed the nearby Bering Land Bridge and became the first occupants of North America. It is therefore likely that the early immigrants to North America were accompanied by large wolf-like animals similar to the dog at Ushki-1.

Native Dogs

During the period of over 10 000 years since their first immigration, the aboriginal dogs of the New World have developed a number of varieties, as different as the sled dog of the north and the tiny Chihuahua of Mexico. Some of these differences probably resulted from interbreeding with local wild canines. Eskimo sled dogs are even today occasionally bred with wolves, so that the breed can maintain its wolf-like size and strength. In more southerly regions, aboriginal dogs must have frequently interbred with coyotes, producing smaller offspring. Other differences probably developed through selective breeding for certain useful characteristics. For example, the Salish peoples of the West Coast bred small woolly dogs and used their hair in weaving clothing and blankets.

While the Salish wool dog was perhaps the most specialized of aboriginal breeds, dogs in other regions of the country were bred for a variety of other tasks. The Eskimo sled dog is the best known and was certainly the breed that contributed most valuably to the lives and economies of its human companions. Pulling heavy loads over vast distances of sea ice was not its only contribution: it also used its sense of smell to locate the hidden breathing holes of seals living beneath the ice; it chased muskoxen into their characteristic defensive stands, which protected them from wolves and dogs but which made them vulnerable to human hunters; and it harried polar bears so that they could be killed by a man with a lance. The dogs of the northern forests also pulled sleds and tracked animals. In addition, the Cree kept a very small breed of white short-haired dog for hunting, and I may have known such a dog in an isolated camp east of James Bay where I worked in the 1950s. The dogs of the Plains Indians were used to drag travois, an arrangement of poles tied together to support a load of family belongings. When horses were obtained during the eighteenth

Dogs and man pull a heavily laden sled across the sea ice of the central Arctic.

century, the travois was adapted to their larger size, and one of the Plains Indian names for the horse means "large dog".

Of all the aboriginal dogs of Canada, only the Eskimo dog of the far north, protected by its isolation, has survived as a distinct breed. Elsewhere, centuries of random interbreeding with dogs imported from abroad has obscured the distinctive characteristics of all other aboriginal breeds. According to the generally unreliable folklore of professional dog breeders, some standard breeds trace part of their ancestry to aboriginal Canadian dogs. Specifically, retrievers are reputed to have been developed during the last century through crosses between European spaniels or setters and the native dogs of eastern Canada. Whether or not this is true, we may be certain that the aboriginal dogs did leave descendants in the contemporary world. Few of them may be found in the show rings of the nation, but they must be well represented among the large population of mixed-breed dogs found in the Indian reserves, camps, farms and villages of rural Canada.

heavy blow, removing a sharp-edged flake of bone (found in another section of the cave) that could have been used as a knife. It seems likely that only a human hand could have delivered such a blow or have carried a cobble larger than a fist from the distant riverbank, perhaps for use as a hammer to break the bones of elephants.

The evidence of Ice Age human activity in the Bluefish Caves, though nebulous, is fairly convincing. These caves are potentially our best hope for proving that humans occupied the New World 5 000 to 10 000 years earlier than has been generally supposed.

CHAPTER 3

PEOPLE OF THE GLACIER'S EDGE

Between 10 000 and 11 000 years ago, southern Ontario was a tundra land on the margins of the retreating glaciers. Palaeo-Indian hunters of caribou explored the country and left the remains of their camps along the shores of ancient lakes.

Reconstruction of a Palaeo-Indian spearhead, made from chipped stone and mounted on a wooden shaft.

Southwestern Ontario today consists of a man-made landscape of rich farmlands. In some areas, plains as flat and treeless as those of central Saskatchewan stretch to a horizon broken by the silhouettes of silos and the skeletons of dead elm trees. Even the brushy fence lines of one-time family farms have been bulldozed to create larger fields that can be more profitably worked by larger machinery. Such machines must have been beyond the imagination of the eighteenth- and nineteenth-century pioneers who cleared this land with axe and fire.

When we think of the original landscape of Ontario, it is natural to imagine it as it was found by these early farmers – a vast and almost trackless sea of trees rolling unbroken from Lake Erie to Georgian Bay. Yet the original landscape of southwestern Ontario, as seen over 10 000 years ago by the first human immigrants, was probably superficially closer to the one we see now than to that of the eighteenth century. If in our minds we cover the stubble and ploughed fields with the first snowfall of November and perhaps hide the silos in a snow squall, and if we are not knowledgeable enough to distinguish the tracks of feedlot cattle from those of caribou or muskoxen, we could well be looking through the eyes of one of the Palaeolithic hunters who lived here at the end of the last ice age.

A Corridor
Between the Glaciers

The previous chapter described Canada during the last ice age, when most of the country lay buried beneath several hundred metres of glacial ice. Early immigrants from Asia could have occupied the unglaciated areas of Alaska and the Yukon, but their route to the south was probably blocked by massive ice-sheets. Intermittently, however, the ice-sheets may have retreated slightly and opened a corridor along the eastern edge of the mountains in the western Northwest Territories and Alberta. It was probably along this corridor, between the continental ice-sheets on the Canadian Shield and the glaciers on the mountains to the west, that the first humans penetrated central North America. We do not know precisely when this migration occurred, but it was probably toward the end of the last ice age, when the glaciers had begun to melt and retreat. We do know that about 12 000 years ago Palaeolithic hunters had spread over much of central and southern North America. As the ice-sheets began to retreat northwards, these people were

in a position to follow them and move into southern Canada.

Southern Ontario was one of the first parts of Canada to be deglaciated. At the height of the Ice Age, about 20 000 years ago, the southern margin of the glacier lay in the Ohio Valley, and sometime between 15 000 and 18 000 years ago this margin began to retreat. About 11 000 years ago the edge of the ice lay to the north and east of Georgian Bay, roughly along the imaginary line today separating southern and northern Ontario. During this retreat much of the geological landscape of southern Ontario was formed. As the glacier melted it dropped its burden of boulders and pebbles and rock dust quarried from the Canadian Shield to the north, creating the sheets of till that form the base of most of Ontario's farmland. Rivers of meltwater, flowing over or through the ice, collected and sorted out the local gravel and sand deposits so useful today to the construction industry. As the rate of melting increased, the area entered a period of immense ice-edge lakes, the forerunners of the present Great Lakes.

A Frozen Sea

Most of southern Ontario was covered at some time by these lakes, and from their turgid waters settled the silts and clays that form the rich soil of today's farms. Under the vast weight of the glaciers, the semiplastic rock of the earth's mantle was pressed downwards, and as the edge of the ice retreated it left a huge basin into which poured rivers of frigid meltwater. To the west, Lake Agassiz covered much of what is now Manitoba and the adjacent northern states. To the east, salt water flowed from the Atlantic into a trough known as the Champlain Sea, which at one time covered much of eastern Ontario and southwestern Quebec. Gravel pits along the shores of this ancient sea have yielded the bones of arctic seals, walrus and whales. Seasonally covered by pack ice, the Champlain Sea must have closely resembled the present Hudson Bay.

The first people to enter Ontario were, like everyone on earth at the end of the last ice age, hunters of the large animals of the period – the Pleistocene megafauna of the palaeontologists. These included not only the large mammals inhabiting northern Canada at present, but also animals now associated only with other parts of the world: horses, bison, camels and, most impressive of all, the mammoth and mastodon, both ancient relatives of today's elephants.

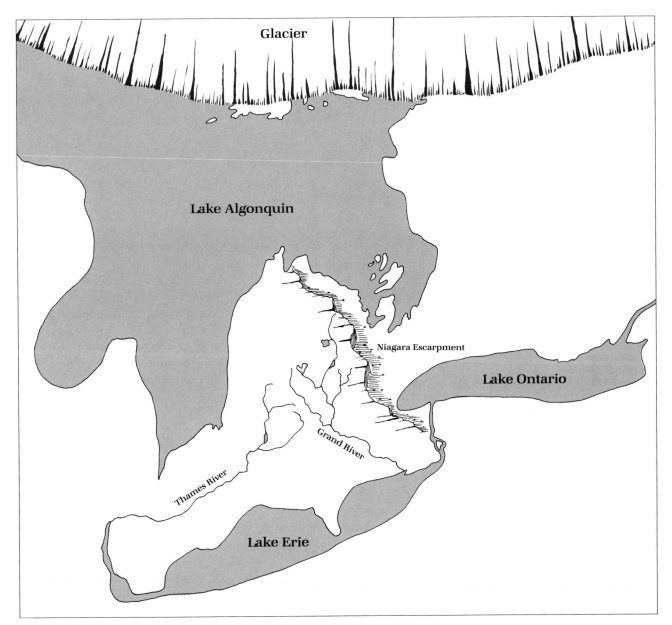

Glacier

Lake Algonquin

Niagara Escarpment

Lake Ontario

Grand River

Thames River

Lake Erie

Southern Ontario as it looked about 11 000 years ago. Glacial meltwater and icebergs poured into Lake Algonquin from the ice-cap to the north, while spruce forests slowly expanded northwards from the area south of Lakes Erie and Ontario. The landscape probably resembled that of the present-day Barren Grounds, west of Hudson Bay.

The landscape of southern Ontario must have seemed generally familiar to the people who had hunted along the southern margin of the continental glaciers for many generations. The white dome of the ice-sheet to the north must have been as familiar, and as unexplored, as was the Inland Ice to the aboriginal Inuit of Greenland. The ice edge itself – massive, tumbling ice cliffs and racing streams, a tumult of noise and barren rock, sterile lakes and chilled air – was doubtless avoided as much as possible, but probably held a prominent place in folklore and legend. Habitable

land began a few kilometres to the south, where caribou and other herbivores grazed on tundra plants established by the seeds and spores that had been carried northwards by winds, rivers and migrating birds.

Easy Prey

It was into such a landscape, perhaps on summer hunts northwards from the edge of the continuous forest, that people from what is now Michigan and Ohio discovered the new land north of Lake Erie. The flat or gently rolling plains they first encountered must have been prime grazing land for Ice Age herbivores. These animals had never seen humans before, and their curiosity must have made them easy prey. In such a situation small groups of hunters, living off the land, could have rapidly explored the new country, leaving their families at well-supplied camps in the

In ancient times, caribou were probably attracted to the shores of glacial lakes, where cold winds from the ice alleviated the discomfort from mosquitoes and biting flies. Rock cairns like the one in the foreground may have been used to channel caribou to where they could be easily killed by men with spears.

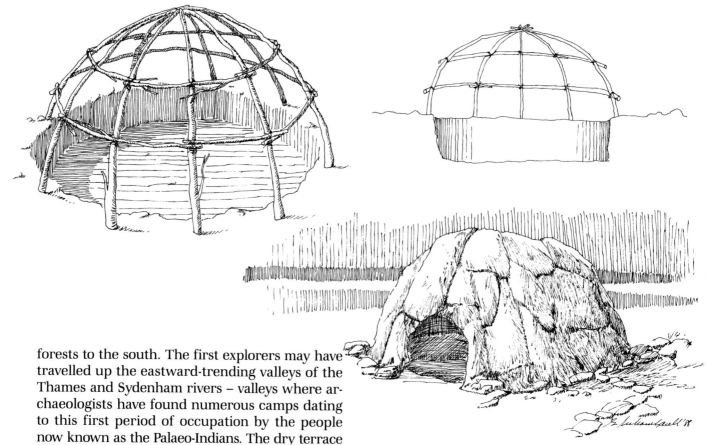

The Palaeo-Indians of the glacier edge probably lived in tents covered with animal skins. Those who spent part or all of the year north of the tree line may have used domed tents supported by thin spruce or alder poles. Traditionally used by several forest-edge Indian and Inuit peoples, tents such as these featured a shallow interior pit, which made them roomier and easier to keep warm.

forests to the south. The first explorers may have travelled up the eastward-trending valleys of the Thames and Sydenham rivers – valleys where archaeologists have found numerous camps dating to this first period of occupation by the people now known as the Palaeo-Indians. The dry terrace edges of the river valleys would have provided easy travelling through the flat and boggy land, while spruce forests growing in the shelter of the valleys would have afforded firewood. The rivers must have been the guides for these earliest explorers, the means of finding their way back home in unknown and unmarked country.

Three or four days of easy walking and hunting up the valley of the Thames River would have brought them to the river forks near present-day London. Another day would have brought them to the area of modern Woodstock and Stratford as they approached a height of land and the headwaters of the river. The first exploration perhaps went no farther. Another summer, however, when the land was well enough known for families to be brought up the valleys to share in the abundant game, hunters may have discovered the Grand River to the east, which ran through another wide and game-filled valley.

An Immense Glacial Lake

A day or two of walking to the east from the middle of the Grand River valley would have brought hunters to the rim of the Niagara Escarpment, the most impressive geological feature of southern Ontario. Modern hikers on the Bruce

Trail know the exhilaration of reaching the edge of the escarpment: streams race down wooded ravines past grazing cattle dwarfed in the patchwork of fields 150 metres below, and far to the east is the glint of Lake Simcoe and Georgian Bay. At the end of the Ice Age the escarpment, a jagged line of limestone cliffs and tumbled blocks, was much starker than at present, its rocky bones still bare of soil and vegetation. The country below would have been uniformly green, and instead of modern cattle there would have been herds of caribou and muskoxen and perhaps a family of grazing mammoths. In the distance were clumps of rolling hills, the moraines moulded by moving glaciers, and to the south the waters of Lake Iroquois, overfilling the present Lake Ontario basin so that the shoreline was at the base of the Casa Loma hill in Toronto. The most impressive feature of the landscape must have been the huge lake, only an hour's walk from the foot of the escarpment and stretching to the northern and eastern horizons.

This was Lake Algonquin, which for close to 2 000 years filled the present basins of Lake Huron and Georgian Bay, and covered much of central Ontario. It must have been an imposing lake, charged by huge rivers of silty meltwater, studded with icebergs carved from the glacier that formed its northern shore, and swept by storms with a fetch of some 300 kilometres over open water. Very unlike the summer-cottage image of the present Lake Huron and Georgian Bay, this lake was certainly not a vacation paradise. Nevertheless, the Palaeo-Indians seem to have chosen the southern shore of the lake as a favoured living area, and the ancient shoreline today serves as a guide to archaeologists searching for sites related to this most ancient period of Ontario prehistory.

One such group of searchers, led by Peter Storck of the Royal Ontario Museum, has over the last decade covered more than 400 kilometres of the ancient shoreline, from east of Lake Simcoe to the town of Collingwood on Georgian Bay. William Roosa, of Waterloo University, and Brian Deller, a schoolteacher who is also a trained amateur archaeologist, have done similar work along the Lake Algonquin beaches of southwestern Ontario. The search, undertaken with the permission of farmers and with as little damage as possible to crops, usually involves an archaeological technique known as field walking – systematic searches of ploughed fields or of fields planted in widely spaced crops such as corn. Strolling through a hot summer cornfield, eyes on the ground in search of fragments of artifacts brought up by the plough, the archaeologist finds it difficult to believe that he is walking the shoreline of an immense glacial lake.

continued page 44

The earliest occupants of Canada were skilled in the difficult and useful art of chipping sharp-edged tools from stone. The by-products of this important activity – hundreds of small flakes and chips of stone – litter the surface of most ancient camp sites.

The Stone Age

Spear point made of native copper obtained from deposits near Lake Superior about 3 500 years ago.

Ground-slate bayonet from a 3 800-year-old burial site in New Brunswick.

When antiquarian Christian Thomsen began organizing the collections of the Danish National Museum in 1816, he did so on the basis of the materials used by various prehistoric peoples for their basic cutting tools and weapons. Danish prehistory was therefore divided into three ages: Stone, Bronze and Iron. In 1865, British prehistorian Sir John Lubbock refined this scheme by subdividing the Stone Age into the Old Stone Age (Palaeolithic), characterized by tools of chipped stone, and the New Stone Age (Neolithic), characterized by ground and polished stone tools. This basic classification system of the past has remained in use to the present day.

The Most Ancient Tools

Because of the hard and chemically inert nature of most stones, tools and weapons made from stone have been preserved in archaeological sites long after implements made from wood, bone or other materials have decayed. We therefore have a preserved record of the gradually evolving use of stone over the past million years. The earliest known tools were simply pebbles struck against other pebbles to knock off flakes and create a sharp edge, which could then be used for butchering animals, scraping hides or cutting wood. By the late Palaeolithic Age of ten to twenty thousand years ago, when ancestral Indians moved into the New World, techniques had advanced greatly.

Like most other human groups of the time, the early Indians were adept at chipping tools from stone. Special hard and fine-grained stones selected for this work must have been eagerly sought by early peoples. Deposits of flint, chert, quartzite and obsidian, a volcanic glass that was the best material for making tools, were mined throughout the New World and were widely traded. These stones, which break much like glass, allowed the craftsman to control the shape of the tool and create extremely sharp cutting edges. Techniques had been developed to make maximum use of small pieces of good stone; from a shaped core of stone, a craftsman could punch off numerous long slivers with parallel edges, much like old-fashioned razors and with as sharp an edge. (Similar

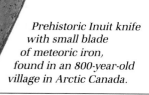

Prehistoric Inuit knife with small blade of meteoric iron, found in an 800-year-old village in Arctic Canada.

Spear point chipped from obsidian (volcanic glass) that originated in Wyoming.

Spear point chipped from stone found only in the Ramah Bay region of far-northern Labrador.

surgical knives have recently been made from glass, which can be given a sharper edge than steel.) These blades were then chipped into a large variety of tools and weapons: spear points, knife blades, drill bits for boring holes, scrapers for working hides, and various cutting and scraping tools for fabricating other tools from wood or bone.

A Sophisticated Technology

Their knowledge of stone deposits, their network of trade routes to distribute high-quality stone, and their skill in chipping this stone into a variety of useful and durable tools were advantages that offset the early Indians' lack of bronze or iron tools and weapons. Within a few thousand years of their occupation of the New World, various groups extended their use of stone by shaping tools through grinding, pecking and polishing. These techniques made it possible for them to use a much greater variety of stones, ranging from limestone to jade, and to make larger implements. Slate was polished, especially by coastal peoples, to form knives

and piercing weapons to hunt sea mammals. Adzes, gouges and chisels with sharp ground edges must have greatly increased the efficiency of woodworking, especially in tasks like the manufacture of dugout canoes. Stone was pecked or carved to produce a variety of containers, most notably the large soapstone pots and lamps of the ancestral Inuit.

The aboriginal peoples of Canada also made use of metal deposits. As early as 6 000 years ago the copper deposits of western Lake Superior had been discovered, and copper was widely traded in the form of tools or weapon points produced by heating the copper nuggets and hammering them into the desired shape. Similar copper deposits in southeastern Alaska and in the Cop-

permine River area of the central Arctic were likewise exploited at a later date. Approximately 1 000 years ago, the ancestral Inuit discovered the large iron meteorites of northwestern Greenland and began to hammer out small iron tools, which were traded across the eastern Arctic. Small quantities of iron, bronze and copper were also obtained by the prehistoric Inuit from the Greenlandic Norse and through trade across the Bering Strait. Soon after reaching Arctic Canada, the ancestral Inuit of this period almost abandoned stone tools in favour of implements with metal cutting edges.

The prehistoric peoples of Canada cannot be characterized simply as having a "stone age" technology, with the implication that their artifacts were crude and inefficient. Most groups did use stone cutting tools, but these tools testify to sophisticated and efficient knowledge and use of materials, skill in working various kinds of stone to produce useful and aesthetically pleasing implements, and the development of effective trade routes to distribute these materials.

Yet the evidence of the ancient lake is there: a bluff 5 to 25 metres high cut by the waves of two millennia of storms, complete with the remains of offshore sandbars, river deltas and other features characteristic of a large body of water. In reconstructing the ancient coast, Storck has noted that the majority of Palaeo-Indian camps were located in areas of complex shorelines – lagoons, bays and peninsulas – rather than on featureless stretches of coast that would provide little shelter from the wind and waves. He has also noted from the local topography that most of the sites had a good view not only of the shore, but of other vistas as well, an important factor to hunters who spent much time observing the surrounding country for game.

Hunters in an Arctic Landscape

Although no animal bones have been found on these sites, we may speculate that the Palaeo-Indians were making some use of the fish resources of the lake. Their main food supply, however, must have been the large herbivores who wandered the early postglacial tundra and forest, and they probably ate caribou most of the year. The caribou were likely attracted to the area near the lake for the same reason that present-day caribou are attracted to arctic coasts: for the cold winds that provide some protection against the immense insect populations of summer tundras. The shore, incidentally, would tend to concentrate the caribou and funnel them past the hunting camps established along the coast.

The present-day caribou of the Barren Grounds west of Hudson Bay follow a seasonal migration of several hundred kilometres, wintering in the spruce forests of northern Saskatchewan and Manitoba and moving north each spring to bear their calves and to feed on the Keewatin tundras. Before the time of the fur trade, the Chipewyan Indians followed the caribou on this yearly round. One piece of archaeological evidence suggests that the movements of the ancient caribou of southern Ontario and their Palaeo-Indian hunters followed a similar pattern. Two of the largest Palaeo-Indian sites to be excavated in the area, the Fisher site near Collingwood (excavated by Storck) and the Parkhill site between London and Sarnia (excavated by Roosa), produced chipped-flint artifacts so similar in style that they could have been made by the same group of people. Moreover, most of the artifacts from the Parkhill site were made from a type of flint known to occur only in the Blue Mountain region near Collingwood. The most likely explanation is that these two sites, 185 kilometres apart, were occupied by the same group of people at different periods in their seasonal round, in which summers were spent on the barren shores of Lake Algonquin and winters in the sheltered spruce forests a week's walk to the south.

Life in an Unpredictable Land

Aside from what we can learn from the locations of their camps and from the broken or abandoned chipped-stone tools, which are all that time has preserved of their technology, we know little about the lives of the Palaeo-Indians who were the first occupants of Ontario. They probably lived throughout the year in skin-covered tents, either conical in shape and supported by straight spruce poles or dome-shaped and supported by bent-over alders, and heated by a central hearth. The women likely prepared the food, gathered firewood, made skin clothing and raised the children; the men would have spent most of their time hunting and making weapons and tools. Each small band, composed of a few related families, probably spent most of their lives together and rarely met other such bands.

By present-day standards it was certainly a hard life, in a relatively unpredictable world: animals required for human survival could appear and disappear for no apparent reason; a familiar ocean-like lake could disappear in a few months, as the retreating glacier or the tilting land opened a new outlet to the sea. There must also have been the exhilaration of a long chase over dry tundra, the peace of summer mornings when the lake was quiet and the food caches full of meat, the excitement and trepidation of moving into unknown country, and the satisfaction of returning to boast the discovery of a new and fruitful land.

Rock cairns such as this one built by Inuit in northern Quebec may have been used by the first caribou hunters to occupy southern Canada.

CHAPTER 4

THE BURIAL-MOUND BUILDERS

On the southern coast of Labrador, between 7 000 and 7 500 years ago, a child was ceremonially buried beneath a large mound of sand and boulders. Such elaborate burial practices are not expected, or elsewhere known, of hunting peoples of the early postglacial period.

Bone flute, or whistle, found with the skeleton at L'Anse-Amour.

Fifteen thousand years ago, almost all the land that is now Canada lay beneath a gleaming dome of glacial ice; yet 7 000 years ago, all that remained of the great continental glaciers were a few small ice-caps on the mountains of the eastern Arctic. The period during which the climate warmed and the glaciers disappeared was one of major environmental change, not only for Canada but for the entire New World.

A Widespread Cultural Tradition

In Canada the zone close to the retreating edge of the glacier was a land of meltwater rivers, shifting glacial lakes, and barren land covered with vegetation that we find today in arctic tundras and northern forests. Between approximately 10 000 and 12 000 years ago, this zone was occupied by Palaeo-Indian hunters of big game – caribou, bison and perhaps occasionally mammoth or mastodon. The way of life described in the previous chapter was not limited to the early immigrants to southern Ontario. As far east as Nova Scotia and as far west as the Peace River country of northern British Columbia, archaeological sites have produced evidence of occupation by Palaeo-Indian peoples who lived in similar ways, and whose chipped-stone tools and weapon points are so alike that they obviously derive from the same cultural tradition.

The Palaeo-Indians who followed the retreating glaciers north into Canada were merely the northern fringe of a big-game hunting population that, from about 12 000 years ago, expanded rapidly over most of the Americas as far south as Patagonia. For the next 2 000 years these hunters continued to follow what appears to have been a relatively stable and successful way of life.

The End of the Large Herbivores

About 10 000 years ago, however, circumstances began to change rather drastically. The climate became increasingly warmer, forests began to grow in areas hitherto open tundra or steppe, and, most important of all, many of the large animal species on which the Palaeo-Indians had previously depended became extinct. The reasons for their disappearance are not understood. These animals had adapted to previous interglacial periods with no apparent trouble, so it is difficult to blame the changing environment of the time. It seems likely that human hunters had a hand in the extinction of these animals, especially those hunters who had learned to make use of mass-hunting techniques, such as driving herds of animals by setting fire to grasslands.

Whatever the cause, about 10 000 years ago the Palaeo-Indians found themselves in a world quite different from that of their ancestors. Gone were the massive herds of horses, camels, giant bison, elephants and other animals that had roamed the endless tundras and steppes covering most of the New World. Instead, the continents were rapidly becoming a mosaic of relatively small environmental zones, each with its own distinctive set of animals and plants. In these new circumstances, the old and relatively uniform Palaeo-Indian way of life became fragmented, as the inhabitants of each local region learned new ways of coping with their environment and exploiting its resources. From this period on, archaeologists can trace the local adaptations that were to develop over hundreds and thousands of years and lead to the various distinctive Indian ways of life that existed at the time of European contact.

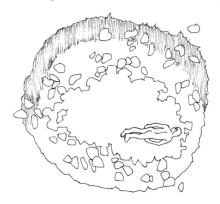

Reconstruction of the burial mound at L'Anse-Amour.

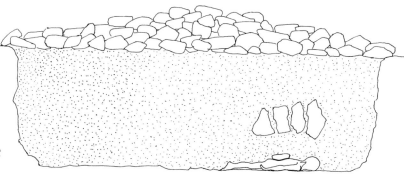

One such local adaptation took place from about 9 000 to 3 000 B.P. on the southern coast of Labrador. Not only is this an unexpectedly long sequence of occupation for such an apparently barren subarctic region, but, as we have found, the early occupants left some remarkable surprises for the archaeologist. The surprises began the day after James Tuck and I arrived on the south coast of Labrador in July 1973. At the time, we both worked at Memorial University of Newfoundland. We had decided to spend a few weeks in the area to investigate archaeological sites that had been known for years, and which we suspected contained evidence of quite early Indian occupation.

The day we arrived was cold, with a dense fog seemingly composed of equal parts water vapour and blackflies. It was late afternoon, too cold and wet to explore and too foggy to see where we were. We set up our tents about a kilometre from the village of L'Anse-Amour, beside a small brook, and in the shelter of a derelict red dump-truck cooked supper in the rain, and went to bed.

The next morning, still in fog, we crossed the gravel road beside our camp and immediately made our first archaeological find. At the edge of the road cut lay a heap of large water-rounded boulders, laid bare by a bulldozer when the road had been built a few years earlier. This appeared to be part of a larger collection of boulders that remained hidden beneath drifted sand and scrub fir beyond the edge of the road cut. The boulders were out of place in this area of sand dunes, but it was unclear who had brought them here or why. Were they part of a structure built by the early Basque or French settlers of this coast? Or were they the remains of a stone house built by the Inuit who occasionally visited the area to trade with or plunder early European fishing stations? Neither of these suggestions made much sense. Because the structure was located several hundred metres from the coast, it must have been buried in scrub, and thus totally inaccessible prior to the recent building of the road. Unable to make sense of the pile of stones, we simply named it "L'Anse-Amour Feature 1", photographed it and left.

Within an hour we had begun to find the archaeological sites that were to keep us busy for the remainder of our stay. Most of them consisted of scatters of chipped-stone tools revealed in sand blowouts; occasionally we could trace thin buried deposits along the edges of the blowouts and, less often, pits or hearth features containing fragments of charcoal and animal bones. The sites were scattered along approximately 50 kilometres of coast, from the town of Blanc-Sablon on the Quebec border northward to the Pinware River. They varied greatly in elevation, some being close to the present shore and others lying up to 27 metres above sea level. Noticing that the styles of artifacts changed with the elevation of the sites, we began to work on the assumption that the sites on higher elevations were older, and had been occupied in early postglacial times when the local land had not yet rebounded from its depression beneath the continental glaciers. This assumption turned out to be correct; radiocarbon dating of samples of charcoal recovered from the various sites indicated that the locations at the highest elevations were occupied between 8 000 and 9 000 years ago, whereas those close to present sea level dated back only about 3 000 years and were thus the most recent Indian sites.

From these findings we began to assemble a picture of the early occupants of this coast. The radiocarbon dates suggested that the first immigrants arrived remarkably early, at a time when a large sheet of glacial ice still covered much of the interior of Labrador and Quebec. The styles of their chipped-stone tools indicated that they were descended from Palaeo-Indian peoples who lived to the south of the Gulf of St. Lawrence. After the draining of the Champlain Sea, some of these people could have crossed to the north shore of the St. Lawrence River, hunting caribou and making some use of coastal resources. Reaching the Strait of Belle Isle area of southern Labrador, they encountered a new resource: the herds of harp seals that whelp on the spring sea ice and are easily hunted with weapons no more sophisticated than clubs and spears. We suspect that it was this abundant resource that encouraged occupation of the locality, and led to a relatively stable way of life that was to last for at least 6 000 years.

A Mysterious Pile of Rocks

Although our work was beginning to result in a vague picture of early Indian occupation of the area, it did not explain the mysterious pile of rocks across the road from our camp, and we left Labrador without learning anything more about the structure. The following summer we returned with a crew of four students, to undertake exca-

The job was to prove long, tedious and initially not very rewarding. We removed over 300 boulders from the upper layers of the mound, and the excavation gradually got larger as the sand walls continued to collapse. However, even when the pit measured seven metres on each side, we had found very little. Beneath the upper layers of boulders lay a deep deposit of fine sand, broken only in one area, where we encountered a vague structure of vertically placed slabs. We thought this might be a cyst surrounding a buried body; however, aside from a few streaks of red ochre and stains of what appeared to be decayed wood or bark, the cyst was empty. Disappointed, we continued with the work, largely because we had already invested so much labour in the project. More importantly, however, because the sand walls of our excavation lacked the fine layering characteristic of water-laid sand, we suspected that we were redigging an ancient excavation.

After another few days' work, we were almost 1.5 metres below the surface and ready to admit that we had wasted our time and effort on a useless pile of rocks. However, just as we were about to give up the work, one of the students, working carefully with trowel and dustpan on the floor of the excavation, found something. It was a small patch of red-stained sand, the deep red one sees on old ochre-painted barns, and reminiscent of the ochre used by the ancient Indians in their burial ceremonies. More trowelling revealed that the ochre-stained sand covered the top of a human skull, and by evening we had revealed most of the skeleton.

Funeral Offerings

There were several surprises that day. For a start, we suspected from the small size of the skeleton that it had belonged to an adolescent, and not a great tribal chief or priest whom we might have expected to be buried with such ceremony. Next there was the unusual position of the body. When people are buried in an extended posture, they are nearly always placed on their backs; this child had been buried in a prone position, face down but with the head turned to one side, and a large slab of rock had been placed on the back. In front of the face lay a walrus tusk, and other grave-offerings were scattered around

vations at some of the sites we had found. One day, when we were digging in another portion of the sand dunes near L'Anse-Amour, we sent some of the students off to clear the brush and sand from our old pile of rocks so that we could get a better look at it.

Once cleared off, the heap of rocks turned out to be much more widespread than we had thought. It was arranged in a roughly circular pattern approximately eight metres in diameter. It was also apparently older than we had thought, for in the uncleared area we could see that the boulders were overlain by drifted sand containing a buried humus layer that we had also found on several sites in the area and that we estimated was formed about 2 000 years ago. In the sand covering the boulders we found one artifact: a large polished whetstone of the kind used by the early Indian occupants of the area. We gradually accepted the fact that our pile of rocks was not the remains of a structure built by Inuit or Europeans during the past few centuries, but that it had been assembled in a much earlier period. Two boulder structures, thought to have covered burials that subsequently disappeared, had been recently reported on the nearby Quebec coast, and we suspected that this was such a burial mound. We shifted all of the students to the site, mapped and photographed the site, and began systematically to remove the boulders and excavate in the underlying sand.

In an imaginative reconstruction, the mound covering the burial at L'Anse-Amour is completed. A drummer, beating on the tambourine-like drum common to northern peoples, sings a shamanic song while a memorial pole bearing the skull of a walrus is raised. Walrus must have been the largest and most dangerous game hunted by this maritime people, and its symbolic importance is suggested by the ivory tusk placed before the face of the buried child.

the body. Several spear points chipped from stone or carved from caribou bone were placed above the head, and there were two stone spear points at the left shoulder. Beneath the chest was a decorated bone pendant, an antler harpoon head, and a bird-bone whistle that, when blown, still produces a sound that makes dogs howl. At the left hip were two nodules of graphite covered with red ochre, and a small decorated antler pestle; these objects, probably originally enclosed in a small skin pouch, may have been a kit for making metallic-red paint. Beneath the other hip was a carved, crescent-shaped ivory object with a hole drilled through the centre, perhaps a toggle for holding the end of a harpoon line. On either side of the body were patches of ash and charcoal, the remains of fires built at the time of burial and then covered as the pit was filled with sand.

Elated by our discovery, we spent a couple of days carefully recording and removing the skeleton and the grave-goods. Then came the hard work of refilling the pit and replacing the rocks, an exercise that gave us great respect for the amount of labour put into the original construction of the burial mound. We worked with long-handled shovels and wheelbarrows; the original excavators had probably dug with pieces of caribou antler, like one that was found in the pit, and probably carried the sand in baskets or other containers of birchbark. We calculated that the original digging, refilling and carrying of boulders from a nearby stream bed would have been a full week's hard work for approximately 20 people.

A 7000-Year-Old Event

Later that fall, back in our laboratory at Memorial University, the surprises continued. Sonja Jerkic, a physical anthropologist, confirmed our suspicion that the skeleton had belonged to a very young person, about 12 or 13 years of age at the time of death and thus too young for the distinctive markings of either sex to be imprinted on the skeleton. Radiocarbon dates, based on samples of charcoal taken from the grave-fires in the bottom of the pit, came back from two laboratories; they agreed in dating the burial between 7 000 and 7 500 years ago. This confirmed our conjectures on its age, which were based on the high elevation of the site above sea level and on the fact that the spear points found in the grave were characteristic of styles from the early part of local occupation. We now had not only a very interesting burial, but an extremely old one as well.

Burial mounds are generally associated with agricultural civilizations, whose dense populations and stable food supply allowed the luxury of large-scale construction projects to protect the dead or preserve the memory of prominent individuals. Dozens of peoples around the world have at various times in human history erected mounds over the bodies of their dead relatives: the Egyptian pyramids, the Megalithic barrows of Europe, the zoomorphic mounds of the central United States and the royal tombs of China are outstanding examples of the practice. But 7 000 years ago, at the time of the L'Anse-Amour burial, the few farming civilizations on earth had not yet developed this idea, and were content to dispose of their dead through simple earth burial or cremation. Yet, on the subarctic coast of Labrador, a small community of hunters and fishermen apparently went to a great deal of trouble to excavate a large pit, bury a child with apparent ceremony, and then erect a rock mound, which must have been a prominent feature of the local landscape. It was surely an unusual burial, for they cannot have had the resources to bury everyone in this manner. Indeed, our searches for similar burial mounds in the area have shown them to be extremely rare.

To suggest the reasons for such an unusual burial, we must rely on imagination rather than on archaeological fact. No child aged 12 or 13 could have reached a position of prominence in a hunting society such as that of the early Indians of Labrador. Perhaps the elaborate burial related not to the life of the individual but to the manner of death. Could this have been a young hunter who had been killed by a walrus or a bear, an event considered so unlucky that it merited unusual ceremony? Or could this have been a sacrificial victim, who was deeply buried, face down, with a rock on the back and covered with tonnes of sand and boulders, in order to lay the ghost? We can never know. Archaeology tells us only that the ancient Indian inhabitants of Labrador, for whatever reason, once went to much effort to provide an unusual burial for a child. It is, in fact, the oldest burial of this scale and complexity known anywhere on earth.

CHAPTER 5

THE FIRST ARCTIC EXPLORERS

The first people to occupy the barren coasts and islands of Arctic Canada came from Asia about 4 000 years ago. Lacking much of the technology of the later Inuit, these people seem to have led lives of terrifying   insecurity.

Found eroding from a sea beach in the High Arctic,
this life-size mask was probably used by a Palaeo-Eskimo shaman.

Four thousand years ago, human populations had spread to almost all regions of the earth; only Arctic Canada, Greenland, Antarctica and a few isolated oceanic islands remained uninhabited. The Canadian Arctic must have looked much as it does today – a jigsaw puzzle of barren peninsulas and islands, several of them larger then Newfoundland, separated by narrow gulfs and channels that remained frozen for most or all of the year. The climate was slightly warmer than now, but summers were not warm enough to support more than the present vegetation of herb tundra in the south and arctic desert in the north. Winters must have been as cold and as long as they are today. On the Arctic mainland, groups of Indian hunters had for millennia pushed north of the tree line, following the summer migrations of the caribou, but most of them appear to have retreated each winter to the shelter of the northern forest. The coasts and islands to the north were habitable, but only by people willing to forego the relative comfort of winter south of the tree line.

A Siberian Origin

The first to accept this challenge came from the west, from Alaska, and ultimately from northeastern Siberia. Archaeological information about the vast Siberian forests is relatively scant, but we do know that most of the area had been occupied by hunting peoples since the end of the last ice age. Five thousand years ago these people had at least distant and indirect contacts with the farming peoples of China to the south and with those of central Asia to the west. Through trade with these regions they acquired metal artifacts, first of bronze and later of iron, and learned such civilized arts as pottery-making.

Despite their distant relationships with more civilized worlds, however, these were northern forest hunters, whose lives resembled those of traditional Indian hunters of the northern Canadian bush. We must imagine them following the herds of wild reindeer north of the tree line each

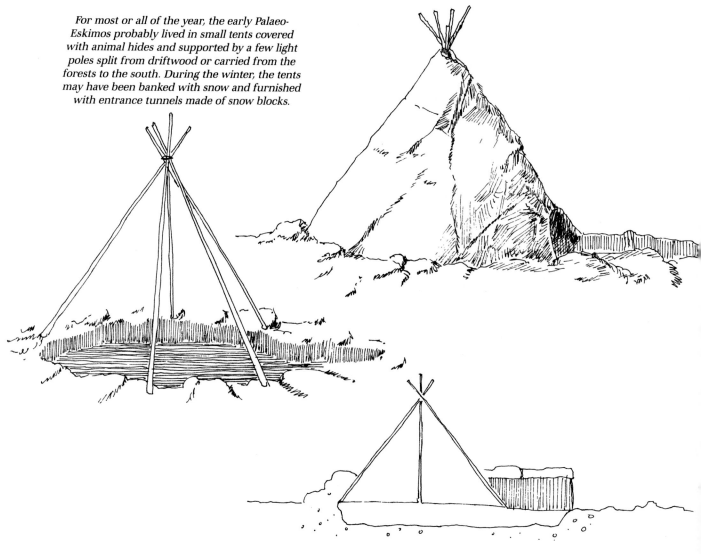

For most or all of the year, the early Palaeo-Eskimos probably lived in small tents covered with animal hides and supported by a few light poles split from driftwood or carried from the forests to the south. During the winter, the tents may have been banked with snow and furnished with entrance tunnels made of snow blocks.

spring and spending the summers in the relatively narrow strip of tundra between the Siberian forests and the Arctic coasts. Here, some of these groups must have discovered the rich sea-mammal resources of the Bering Sea and adapted the sea-hunting technology of more southern peoples to the hunting of arctic seal and walrus. The next step would have involved deciding whether to winter on this northern coast, living on stores of reindeer meat and on the meat and fat of sea mammals killed during the summer or hunted during the dark days of winter. Such a decision eventually led to the first settling of Arctic Canada. Within a very few centuries the descendants of these people spread across the frozen waters of Bering Strait to the coastal plains of Alaska, then eastwards along the coast and through the islands of Arctic Canada as far as Greenland.

A Strong and Gentle Race

We know very little about these first Arctic people, referred to by archaeologists as Palaeo-Eskimos. Physically, they probably resembled Eskimos or the Eskimo-like peoples of northeastern Siberia. They may have spoken a language of the Eskimo family or a related language that has not survived to the present day. Their descendants occupied Arctic Canada for at least 3 000 years, disappearing between 500 and 1 000 years ago when the ancestral Inuit (as the Eskimos of Arctic Canada and Greenland prefer to be named) began to move eastward from Alaska. They have survived in Inuit legend as a strong and gentle race, driven from their Arctic homelands by the Inuit invaders. Some of their inventions were adopted by the Inuit, and some of their people may have been absorbed into early Inuit communities.

The way of life developed by these early Palaeo-Eskimos, a way that allowed them to live year-round on the Arctic coasts and tundras, was something quite new in human history but was nevertheless based on an old cultural pattern. From their Siberian homelands they brought the bow and arrow, previously unknown in the New World. They killed sea mammals with harpoons attached to retrieving lines (weapons developed by North Pacific hunters or Siberian lake-fishermen), and they used barbed bone spears for fishing and hunting birds. Skins for clothing were prepared with scrapers chipped from flint, cut with razor-like flakes of flint called microblades (made according to an ancient Old World technique), and sewn with tiny bone needles.

The floor plan of their tents also seems to have been based on an old Eurasian pattern that survived until recently among the Saame (Lapps) of northern Europe: a central box-hearth forms part of a corridor down the centre of the tent, flanked on either side by working or sleeping areas. In Saame tents the hearth and the edges of the corridor were built of logs, but the Palaeo-Eskimos of Arctic Canada fashioned them from slabs of rock. On undisturbed Arctic beaches these small stone structures can be found today, some of them intact and looking as if they had been built 4 rather than 4 000 years ago.

Undisturbed Remains

These isolated, simple and practically undisturbed ruins are a pleasure and a challenge to the archaeologist. In more southerly regions,

continued page 61

The stillness of the arctic night, lit only by the
northern lights, is broken as the dogs discover a
small herd of muskoxen that has wandered close
to the camp. This disturbance would have been
welcomed in a Palaeo-Eskimo camp. Held in a
circular defence formation by the dogs,
muskoxen would be easy prey to hunters with
bows and spears, and several animals could be
killed. Such a hunt could provide the tiny camp
with weeks of food, heavy muskox robes for
bedding, and bones to supplement the scarce
fuel for heat and light.

A Weapon from the North

The American Indians are often thought of as the preeminent archers of the world. The Indian with his bow and arrow is a familiar figure from history and in the movies. It is surprising, therefore, to learn that the use of the bow began only relatively recently in the New World.

We do not know in how many different places the bow was invented. A projectile point that was once used on a light spear cannot easily be distinguished from one that tipped an arrow. Furthermore, archaeological remains of early arrow points are rare. Those made from hardwood or bone would not have survived in the ground, and the prehistoric use of bows and arrows can be traced mainly through recovered arrowheads made from stone or metal.

The bow was probably first invented in the Old World shortly after the last ice age. The first Indians to reach North America had already crossed to the New World by that time and, like their Palaeolithic relatives in the Old World, hunted exclusively with hand-thrown spears and lances. The earliest certain introduction of the bow to North America was by the early Palaeo-Eskimos, who probably moved across the Bering Strait from Siberia shortly before 2000 B.C., bringing with them an Asiatic archery technology.

At an archaeological site in far-northern Labrador, James Tuck of Memorial University has excavated the remains of early Palaeo-Eskimo occupations dating to approximately 1800 B.C. and containing numerous tiny, chipped-stone arrow points. Other stratigraphic levels of the site, dating to about the same period, contain the remains of occupation by Maritime Archaic Indians, whose distant ancestors built the burial mound at L'Anse-Amour. These layers, however, contain something new in Maritime Archaic technology: small chipped-stone projectile points that appear to be crude copies of Palaeo-Eskimo arrowheads. Tuck has suggested that once the Labrador Indians adopted bow-and-arrow technology from their Palaeo-Eskimo neighbours, it could have spread south and west across the remainder of the

Copper Inuit archers during the early twentieth century. The bow is of the Asiatic pattern introduced to Arctic North America by ancestral Inuit.

New World. This hypothesis fits the dates recorded for the introduction of the bow into other regions of Canada. There is no valid evidence of the weapon's use in either eastern Canada or the Plains area before the first millennium B.C.

Advances in Asiatic bow technology continued to cross the Bering Strait to the New World. When ancestral Inuit moved eastwards from Alaska about 1 000 years ago, they brought with them a compound bow, more complex than other North American bows and very similar to that used by the Mongols when they fought their way to the gates of Europe. Contrary to popular belief, therefore, the use of the bow and arrow in the New World may have been primarily dependent on the Old World contacts of the Eskimos.

where larger populations have lived continuously over the millennia, the remains of past human activity are usually jumbled – the more recent piled on top of the earlier, the earlier dug up and disturbed by the more recent. The whole deposit is tumbled by the root throws of fallen trees, the burrowing of animals and the sluice of running water. Most objects not made of stone, ceramic or other durable materials, are lost through dissolution. Interpreting such complex remains is a trial of logic aided by guesswork. In most cases the archaeologist can only try to reconstruct the general pattern of life of the entire community that left the remains – the daily life of any individual or family in that community is lost in the ground.

In contrast, an archaeological site from the early Palaeo-Eskimo period represents the remains of a much more limited and less complex settlement. Each isolated feature marks the location of a tent, probably occupied by a single family and usually for a period of only a few days or a few weeks. Once the tent was removed, the site was abandoned, often never to be used again.

The Arctic is so large, and Arctic populations so small, that many sites have been undisturbed by later human activities. One reason for this is that, throughout most of the Arctic Archipelago, islands depressed for thousands of years beneath the weight of glacial ice have been rising relative to sea level since deglaciation. Strips of gravel beach forming the shoreline 4 000 years ago have now risen to as much as 50 metres above sea level and are found as fossil beaches far inland from the present coast. Since most prehistoric Arctic hunters camped along the shoreline of the day, the archaeological remains of their camps are now found on these ancient beaches. As a result, many sites have been preserved from later disturbance, for within a generation or two after a site was abandoned it was no longer on the current shore and was therefore less attractive as a campsite. Aside from the occasional trampling by caribou or muskoxen, there are almost no signs of disturbance. Knowing that a 3 500-year-old site is usually found on beaches a few metres lower in elevation than a 4 000-year-old site allows archaeologists to roughly date settlements by their elevations.

The nutrients from decaying bones and other material left in the camp generally support a light vegetation mat of tiny Arctic flowers – heather, saxifrage or poppies – and on the barren beaches

of the High Arctic desert, each ancient camp is marked by its own isolated patch of colourful vegetation. Beneath this mat, the thin earth remains frozen for most or all of the year, so that decay is extremely slow and artifacts of bone, ivory and wood are often perfectly preserved. On the gravel beach in front of one of these camps, I once found the remains of a fox's paw, bleached white, but with each tiny bone remaining in place after 4 000 years.

Each of these sites is a miniature time capsule representing the activity of a few people for a few days or weeks several thousand years ago. In some ruins we can detect patterns of family life: sewing needles are concentrated on the left side of the central passages, whereas weapons and other tools that would have been used by men are concentrated on the right, suggesting that the central corridors divided the areas used by men and women. From slight differences in the styles of chipped-stone tools, as well as substantial differences in the skill applied, we can even detect the work of individual craftsmen within a small community.

The animal bones recovered from the tent sites, and from the small midden areas in front of them where refuse was thrown, give a fair idea of the quantity and type of the family's food. In some areas, especially in the High Arctic islands, the early Palaeo-Eskimos concentrated on hunting muskoxen, whereas in other areas they depended primarily on seals. In some camps the majority of bones are from small game, ducks and Arctic fox, suggesting a season of scarcity and hard times for the people living in the tents.

A Limited Technology

Although we can occasionally gain intimate glimpses of individuals or families, the larger patterns of their lives remain very much a mystery. This is primarily because of what is missing from their archaeological remains, rather than because of what we find. Many of the technological items that were used by the later Inuit occupants of the area, which we generally consider necessary to an Arctic hunting way of life, seem to have been unknown to these earliest immigrants. For example, they do not seem to have used boats, and they had no float harpoons for hunting large sea mammals. This must have restricted them to shore or ice-edge hunting of sea mammals that, when harpooned, could be held by a hand line rather than attached to a float or drag, as in the later Inuit manner of hunting walrus and whale. There is no evidence that they had sled dogs, and only scant evidence that they even had dogs for use in hunting.

They had no oil lamps for winter heat and light, nor is there any evidence that they used the domed snow house that provided winter protection to the later Inuit. All of their heat and light seems to have come from tiny open fires in the central hearths of their tents. These fires were fuelled by small twigs of heather and Arctic willow, occasional chips of driftwood and the bones and fat of the animals that they hunted. Such open fires could not have been used in snow houses, and it seems likely that throughout the year they lived in tents, which were probably insulated by banked snow during the winter. The small amounts of charcoal and burned bone recovered from the hearths suggest that fires may have been occasional luxuries and that the tents were unheated for much of the time. When we consider that winters in Arctic Canada have not changed much over the past 4 000 years and that temperatures then as now must have hovered around −30°C for months on end during the long winter nights, it is difficult to imagine how these people survived.

Many probably did not survive. In the small local groups of three or four families, which the clusters of tent remains suggest were the usual camp group, an accident or illness affecting one or two hunters would have been a very serious matter. Unusually heavy or unusually open sea-ice conditions that interfered with the hunting of sea mammals, or a winter ice-storm that depleted the local caribou and muskox populations by covering their pastures with ice, would have been disastrous. Time and again, local groups must have faced the choice of staying in their camps and starving, or of moving as rapidly as possible to another area that might supply a new source of food.

Highly Mobile Groups

The picture that emerges is of a series of small and very mobile groups, gradually spreading to form a thin network of human occupation across the Arctic as they moved in search of locales that would supply sufficient food to get them through the next winter. There must also have been other attractions leading to the exploration of new islands and new regions: animals

An antler wand excavated from a Dorset village in the High Arctic is carved with 60 faces. Some appear to portray humans, while others may represent spiritual beings. The middle portion of the wand is worn smooth, as if habitually held or carried.

62

continued page 64

The Art
of an Extinct
People

Among the fallen hearth stones and the fragments of broken bones scattered about ancient Palaeo-Eskimo camps lie occasional lost or discarded pieces of art. In the camps of the early Palaeo-Eskimos, these are usually tools of chipped flint – arrow heads and the blades of cutting implements. But they are different from the tools left behind by other Stone Age peoples, whose handiwork seems to have been confined to the most useful tools made from the most easily available stone. In contrast, the Palaeo-Eskimo artisans chose brightly coloured, glass-like stones and chipped them with a skill and care practically unsurpassed anywhere in the world. The artifacts are symmetrically formed, with decoratively serrated edges, and are so small that they appear to be toys, tiny miniatures of the clumsy tools produced by most prehistoric craftsmen. The fabrication of such exquisitely small and jewel-like artifacts must have been considered an art form. It was perfectly suited to the meagre and nomadic lives of the Palaeo-Eskimos and is welcome evidence that these people had the time and the will to delight in fashioning objects of beauty. We occasionally find traces of more sophisticated Palaeo-Eskimo artistic activity in the form of objects carved from bone or ivory. These are rarely preserved in early sites, and it is only in the settlements of later Palaeo-Eskimos that the full range of their carvings is recovered. The descendants of the early Palaeo-Eskimos, known as the Dorset people, occupied Arctic Canada until about 1 000 years ago, when they were either killed or driven away by the invading ancestors of the Inuit. The numerous carvings left by the Dorset people not only reveal one of the most unusual and sophisticated artistic traditions of a prehistoric hunting society, but also provide a unique look at the artistic and religious lives of an extinct people.

Shamanic Art

The art of the Dorset people closely reflects their religious ideas. Masks carved from driftwood and painted with ochre were probably used by shamans in rituals for curing illness, controlling the weather and ensuring successful hunting. Sets of ivory animal teeth, designed to be held in the mouth, must have been used in other ceremonies, in which the shaman transformed himself into an animal, perhaps a bear. Small figures of animals, particularly bears, carved with designs of the skeleton of the animal, may have represented the spirit helpers of the shaman. Miniature harpoon heads may have been magical weapons; figures of humans and animals with holes in the chest, sometimes containing a sliver of wood, were probably used to carry out killings by magic. Wands made of antler are covered with up to 60 carved faces, human and semi-human, perhaps representing the spirits of a community's dead, or a Palaeo-Eskimo pantheon.

A Complex World View

The problems of interpreting Dorset art are similar to those encountered in interpreting the cave paintings of Palaeolithic Europe. Both artistic traditions reveal a level of skill and aesthetic refinement not normally associated with prehistoric hunters. Both indicate a view of the world that is obviously thoughtful, sophisticated and very different from our own. We may never understand the hidden meanings in these alien art traditions, but we are privileged to feel a bond of human recognition and communication across the millennia.

that had never seen humans and were therefore easy prey, and perhaps the suspicion that somewhere in these unknown lands lay a country richer than the one they knew.

It may be inaccurate to picture such a severe way of life for the early Palaeo-Eskimos, a life more meagre and less secure than that of any of the peoples hitherto described by historians and ethnographers – a life that makes the lives of the aboriginal Inuit look positively comfortable by comparison. On the other hand, this picture may be essentially correct, and there may have been people who chose the hazards and discomforts of such a life in order to explore and settle the unknown regions of the Arctic. If so, Arctic Canada holds the archaeological records of a unique human experience, involving not only the exploration of the last great unknown region of the habitable world, but also a way of life in which human needs and comforts were reduced to a level unknown on earth at any other time.

CHAPTER 6

BUFFALO HUNTERS

For up to 10 000 years, from the time of the Palaeo-Indians until the past century, the Indians of the northwestern plains hunted bison by driving them over cliffs. The deep piles of bones and tools that have accumulated on these sites present an archaeological record of   man and bison over the millennia.

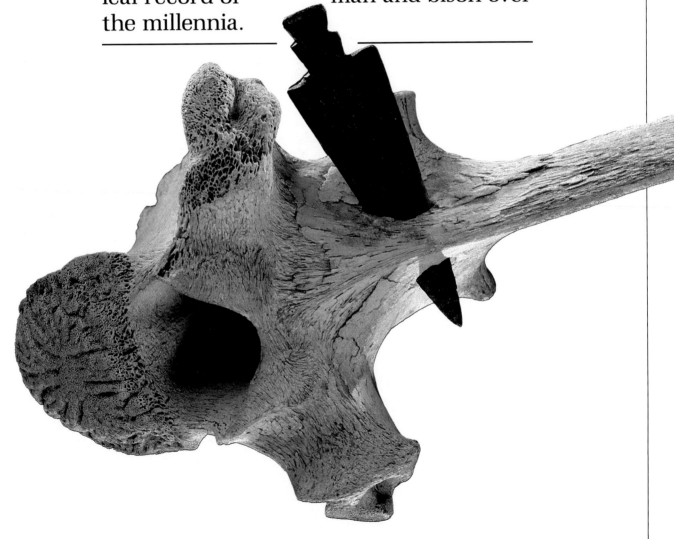

This bison vertebra, found in the Cypress Hills of southern Saskatchewan, was pierced with an iron arrowhead during a nineteenth-century hunt.

The Canadian Plains, as a northern extension of the American West, have a more secure place in the mythology of the modern world than does any other region of Canada. People from all over the world know this country from a thousand Western movies and from the novels that gave rise to the genre. Two vital elements of the Western myth are the Indian and the buffalo. According to the reports of early European travellers, the buffalo roamed the plains in countless numbers. The great herds covered the grasslands as far as the eye could see, stalling trains for hours or days as they shambled across the tracks on their mysterious journeys.

The buffalo fell prey to the Indians, swift-riding bowmen cutting into the herds and killing so easily that they could spend most of their time in the more exciting pursuits of war. The buffalo was central to the Indian way of life; its flesh provided food, its hide was used for clothing and robes and tipi covers, and its dung provided fuel on the treeless plains.

At the Heart of Plains Life

Parts of the myth are true. The buffalo was the basis of life for most Plains Indian groups. Their numbers, however, were greatly exaggerated; this became apparent when the introduction of the repeating rifle led to their virtual extinction within only a few decades. Although large herds did exist, many early accounts make it clear that a traveller could go for days or weeks without seeing a single animal. Hunting the buffalo was therefore not a simple matter, but demanded a great store of knowledge regarding where the animals were likely to be found in any season of

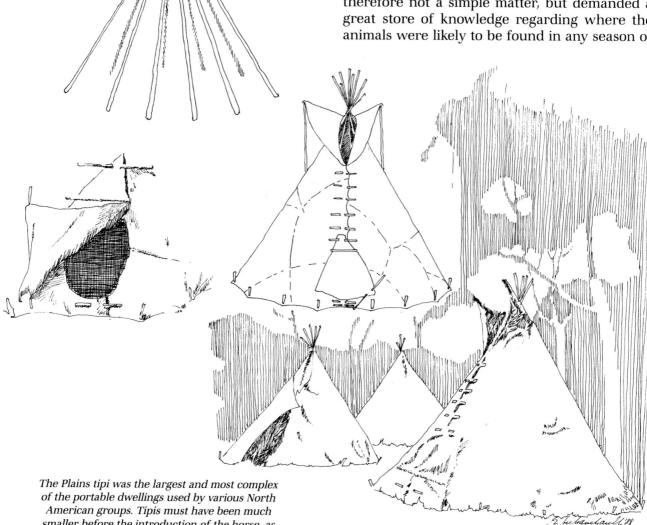

The Plains tipi was the largest and most complex of the portable dwellings used by various North American groups. Tipis must have been much smaller before the introduction of the horse, as the poles and skin covering would have had to be moved from camp to camp on the backs of people and dogs.

the year. It also required skill in getting close to the animals, since neither the lance nor the bow was an effective weapon at more than very short range. The Plains Indians of the nineteenth century had largely solved the latter problem by breeding fast horses and training skilled riders; this technique, however, was a relatively recent introduction to the area. Horses, first obtained from the Spanish colonies in the American Southwest, reached the northwestern plains only in the early eighteenth century. Even after that time, northern groups such as the Blackfoot and the Cree had so few horses that traditional methods of hunting on foot remained the basis of their subsistence.

Buffalo have been clocked at speeds of over 50 kilometres per hour. They possess a keen sense of smell and are wary of humans. Obviously, they cannot be run down or surrounded by human hunters on foot. One traditional method of hunting involved stalking by an individual hunter, often disguised in a wolf skin. Taking advantage of the animals' poor eyesight, keeping downwind and sliding through the tall summer grass, such a stalk could take hours and might yield one, or at most a few, buffalo. Winter hunting was easier; buffalo could be driven into gullies filled with drifted snow, where the floundering beasts were at the mercy of snowshoed hunters.

A More Effective Technique

By far the most productive hunting technique, however, was the drive, in which herds were lured or chased into a position where they could be ambushed. On the level prairie, the ambush usually took the form of a corral or pound constructed of poles and brush in a small valley where it could not be seen by the approaching herds. In the northwestern plains and foothills, where timber was scarce and the land uneven, the ambush more often took the form of a jump – a cliff or steep cutbank over which the herds were stampeded. Suitable locations for such

continued page 72

Traditional Plains Indian tipi camp.

Long-horned bison are stampeded to the edge of a jump by hunters waving skins.

An Essential Invention

Humans are the only animals to wear clothing, but we do not know when the practice began. Since clothing is rarely preserved in the ground, its history has been largely unavailable to archaeologists. From other evidence, however, we can be fairly certain about three aspects of its early history. First, clothing had been invented by the early part of the last ice age, when humans lived for the first time in Europe and Asia under glacial climatic conditions. Second, the first clothing must have been made from animal skins, the only material widely available to our early ancestors that could provide protection from rain and cold. And third, sometime very early in its history, the fabrication of clothing was assigned to women. This last deduction is based on the fact that, until the Industrial Revolution and the more recent invention of European fashion houses, clothes everywhere in the world were designed and made by women. The care of clothing in the average household today still reflects a sexual division of labour that was established at least 50 000 years ago.

The first women to come to North America brought with them the knowledge, developed over countless generations, of how to process animal skins into various kinds of fur and leather, and how to cut and sew these skins to clothe their families. Although we have found no archaeological trace of the clothing they made, we know that the New World would never have been inhabited without their skill in providing protection against the winter weather of a northern latitude during an ice age.

A Complicated Process

The transformation of animal skins into clothing is a complex process: simply skinning an animal and using its hide as protection from the cold produces an object that, on drying, becomes as stiff as a board and has less insulation. If leather is to be produced, an animal skin must be carefully and tediously scraped to remove both the inner layers of the skin and the outer fur. That bone and stone scrapers designed for this task are among the objects most often found in archaeological sites demonstrates the importance of skin-working among prehistoric peoples. The skin must be processed chemically with urine or animal fats to break down the fibres that harden a dry skin. Finally, it must be cleaned, dried, smoked and softened to produce a fur or leather from which clothing can be cut. The clothing of most aboriginal Canadians was made from animal skins that had been subjected to such a process. Only the peoples of the Northwest Coast used other types of clothing, woven from cedar bark or from the wool of mountain goats or domestic dogs.

Early European explorers were probably correct in judging most Canadian Indian clothing to be inadequate for the climatic conditions in which the people lived. Throughout most of aboriginal Canada, women dressed in moccasins, short skirts, and skin capes or blankets; men dressed in moccasins, breechclouts or leggings, and capes or blankets. More adequate clothing was worn by the peoples of the northern forests and must have been available to those living farther south. However,

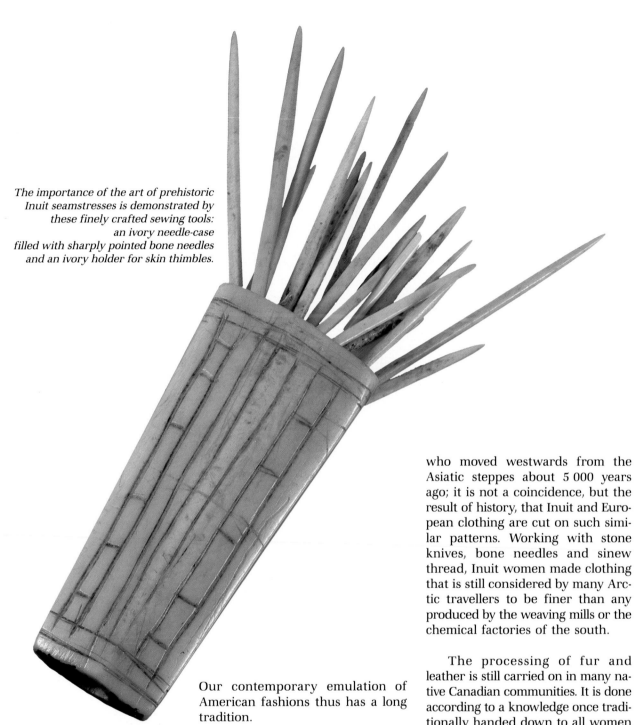

The importance of the art of prehistoric Inuit seamstresses is demonstrated by these finely crafted sewing tools: an ivory needle-case filled with sharply pointed bone needles and an ivory holder for skin thimbles.

one suspects that the style of aboriginal Canadian clothing was greatly influenced by clothing fashions emanating from the warmer regions of what is now the United States. In emulation of more-southern styles, the body was painted and tattooed with decorations that would have been hidden by sensible clothing.

Our contemporary emulation of American fashions thus has a long tradition.

The Finest Seamstresses

Among aboriginal Canadian women, the finest seamstresses were probably found among the Arctic Inuit. Relatively recent immigrants to the New World, they brought with them patterns of tailored clothing that were developed in Asia during the previous few thousand years. These patterns are similar to those brought to Europe by the peoples who moved westwards from the Asiatic steppes about 5 000 years ago; it is not a coincidence, but the result of history, that Inuit and European clothing are cut on such similar patterns. Working with stone knives, bone needles and sinew thread, Inuit women made clothing that is still considered by many Arctic travellers to be finer than any produced by the weaving mills or the chemical factories of the south.

The processing of fur and leather is still carried on in many native Canadian communities. It is done according to a knowledge once traditionally handed down to all women by their mothers, but since forgotten in most of the world. Furs are now produced for the luxury market, but leathers are made largely for moccasins and dance costumes used within aboriginal communities. The leathers can be as soft as cotton and supple as silk, and they retain the subtle smoky odour that, for anyone who has spent time in a traditional native household, smells of comfort and home.

jumps were relatively scarce, and some of the better ones were used for centuries or even millennia. The resulting heaps of buffalo bones became features of the landscape in the Canadian Plains and, in the late nineteenth and early twentieth centuries, a source for the fertilizer industry. The depredations of this industry destroyed many of the sites.

One of the better-known buffalo jumps lies near Cayley, Alberta, about 80 kilometres south of Calgary. Hidden beneath lush grass nourished by many tonnes of decaying bones, it was missed by the fertilizer diggers. It was discovered only in 1952, when a flash flood cut a gully through the site and spread buffalo bones across the prairie. News of the find soon came to the attention of the

Glenbow Foundation of Calgary, which carried out excavations in 1958 and 1959 under the direction of Richard Forbis, now of the University of Calgary. The site was identified as the Old Women's Buffalo Jump, so named because it was reputed to have been used by a tribe of women (who, in Blackfoot legend, lived separately from the men). The adjective "old" refers to the age of the jump, not of the women.

The topography of the Old Women's Buffalo Jump and the masses of bone recovered from the site indicate that it must have been a very successful place to hunt buffalo. An aerial photograph of the site shows a wide expanse of level plain extending westwards toward the mountains; in the foreground, the plain suddenly drops over an 8-metre sandstone cliff to the small valley of Squaw Coulee. The plains to the west must have provided good grazing for buffalo, especially in

In this early-nineteenth-century painting by Peter Rindisbacher, two hunters disguised in wolf skins approach a bison herd.

winter, when chinook winds poured over the tops of the ranges and licked the snow from the landscape. When a hunt was to be held, the young men would have quartered this area on foot, locating a sizeable herd and gently moving it eastwards across the undulating grassland. With the prevailing winds from the west, they could have moved the herd simply by staying behind it and letting the animals catch their scent, directing it by occasionally moving up on either side.

As the herd approached Squaw Coulee, after hours or days of slow travel, the animals would have begun to notice objects on either flank – occasional piles of brush and boulders set in converging lines and designed to direct their drifting path towards the ambush ahead. With increasing unease, they would have begun to trot and then to gallop, as hidden men emerged from the drift fences and began the serious chase. Such escape

behaviour is contagious in a buffalo herd, and when the animals in front found themselves on the edge of the cliff they would not have been able to turn back, but would inevitably have been pushed over by the stampeding masses behind. Hurtling from the height of a three-storey building to the hard earth below, broken-legged and crushed by falling bodies, they were easy prey to hunters with bows and lances. The scene of the kill is evoked by the Blackfoot name for such a killing place: *piskun*, meaning deep blood kettle.

Since Before the Time of Christ

The excavations at the site revealed masses of buffalo bones extending over 30 metres along the base of the cliff and over 60 metres downslope from it. In places, the bone beds and the lenses (lenticular layers) of broken and charred bone

Notched spear point of the type used by Plains hunters about 2 000 years ago.

extend more than four metres below the present soil level. Mixed with the bones were the weapons and tools of the hunters: over 1 000 chipped-stone points of lances and arrows, a few heavy stone choppers for breaking bones, stone knives for skinning the animals and cutting up the meat, a handful of potsherds and a single black bead carved from soapstone. The styles of the weapon points changed gradually from the lower to the upper layers, indicating that the jump had been used over a period of centuries rather than merely years or decades. A sample of burned bone from one of the lower levels produced a radio-carbon date of about A.D. 120, and it seems likely that the jump had been used from before the time of Christ until shortly before the arrival of Europeans in the area. Throughout this period of almost 2 000 years the young men of local groups sought out the herds and drove them to the "deep blood kettle" to be dispatched by the hunters, the women cooked the meat and sewed the hides into clothing – and the bones piled up. Over the centuries an entire human way of life developed, based on the animals whose bones are collected in such dense heaps here and at hundreds of other jumps and pounds scattered across the prairies and plains. Recently, the largest buffalo jump known in Canada, the Head-Smashed-In Buffalo Jump near Fort Macleod, became the second Canadian archaeological site listed on Unesco's list of World Heritage Sites.

CHAPTER 7

BUILDERS OF THE SERPENT MOUND

About 2 000 years ago, on the hills of central Ontario, a serpentine mound 60 metres long was built as a burial structure. The ideas behind such earthworks emanated from the Hopewell culture of the Ohio Valley and ulti-   mately from the civilizations   of Mexico.

Earspools, designed to fit through a hole in the earlobe, were worn by the classical Maya of Central America and contemporaneous peoples of highland Mexico. This specimen from an archaeological site in southern Ontario is evidence of a fashion that spread northwards from the civilizations far to the south.

Highway 7, the shortest route between Ottawa and Toronto, is heavily travelled by truckers and lovers of scenery who shun the faster four-lane expressway to the south. The old highway also gives the traveller a chance to see in one tour much of the geological history of Ontario. Heading west out of Ottawa, it cuts a straight line across the flat bed of the Champlain Sea, an arm of the Gulf of St. Lawrence where 10 000 years ago seals and whales swam among the ice floes above what is now valuable farmland. Then the road begins to climb and twist through the swamps and red rock outliers of the Canadian Shield, formed from some of the oldest rocks on earth. After about 100 kilometres of cliffs, trees and sharp curves, the rocks recede and the road begins to wind through a landscape resembling a giant's sandbox, sculpted and moulded from material carried within the glaciers of the last ice age. Most prominent are the drumlins – hundreds of long, narrow hills oriented in the same direction, all with gradual northern slopes ending in steep south-facing bluffs. The drumlins, serpentine eskers and round, steep kames are so regularly shaped that one is tempted to view them as ancient constructions by a race of intelligent giants.

Man-Made Mounds

It is not surprising, therefore, to learn that nestled among the glacial mounds and hills are a few large earth structures that were built by an intelligent race, not giants but the ancestors of the Canadian Indians. A few kilometres east of Peterborough a highway sign points the way to Serpent Mounds Provincial Park. The park is centred on a drumlin that forms a rounded point on the north shore of Rice Lake. On the flat top of the drumlin, in a grove of oak trees, lies a group of nine artificial earth mounds. Eight of the structures are round or oval, up to 15 metres across and rising half a metre to a metre above the surrounding surface. The ninth structure, named the Serpent Mound by nineteenth-century investigators, is one of the most impressive prehistoric constructions in Canada. Approximately 60 metres long and 8 metres wide, with its rounded back rising between one and two metres above the surrounding ground, it resembles an undulating serpent.

The first recorded excavations in the Serpent Mound were by David Boyle, sent to the site in 1896 by the Ontario government. Boyle reported that the mounds had already suffered extensively from "the morbid depredations of diggers anxious merely to lay bare human remains or to possess a skull". Such depredations continued after Boyle's time, and were brought to a halt only in 1955 when the area was protected as a provincial park. When it established the park, the Ontario government commissioned extensive archaeological investigation of the site; this was carried out by the Royal Ontario Museum and directed by Richard Johnston, a professor at Trent University in nearby Peterborough until his recent death. As a result of this work, we can piece together a vague history of the Serpent Mound and the people who built it.

About 2 000 years ago, Southern Ontario was occupied by Indians who probably spoke languages of the Algonquian or Iroquoian families, or perhaps both. Their ancestors had settled the area thousands of years before and had seen the changes in the shape and size of the Great Lakes as the land slowly twisted and rose. More recently, they had seen gradual alteration of the forests as the postglacial climate changed to conditions somewhat like today's. By the time the Rice Lake mounds were built, the environment had been relatively stable for generations, and each local Indian band must have known their area and its resources as well as a modern Ontario farmer knows his fields. Their year was probably divided among a series of seasonal camps, each located so as to enable the exploitation of local resources such as a spring fish-run, an autumn passenger-pigeon roost, or a winter deer-yard. The site on Rice Lake seems to have been used as a summer camp, and the extensive midden of shells located near the mounds suggests that at this season the people depended heavily on freshwater mussels.

Influences from the South

Although most of the Woodland Indians of 2 000 years ago probably went through their entire lives without meeting more than a few hundred people, they were not entirely isolated from developments elsewhere in the world. For thousands of years their ancestors had received small quantities of exotic goods through trade, including native copper from the Lake Superior region and sea shells from as far away as the Atlantic coast and the Gulf of Mexico. Within the previous few generations, the use of pottery cooking vessels had been introduced through contacts with peoples to the south of the Great Lakes. Such contacts spread ideas as well as material goods.

continued page 83

Burial Rites

Although other animals grieve over their dead companions, humans are the only animals to have developed ritual means of disposing of their dead. The first archaeological evidence of purposeful burial comes from early in the last ice age, about 70 000 years ago, when an early form of human known as *Homo sapiens neandertalensis* occupied much of Europe and western Asia. "Neanderthal Man", named from a skeleton excavated during the last century in the Neander Valley of Germany, was not the low-browed primitive imbecile portrayed by modern cartoonists. The Neanderthals did occasionally live in caves and had massive facial sinuses that produced a broad ridge of bone across their eyebrows, but they may have had as much brain power as most humans living today. In fact, according to the measurements of excavated skulls, the average Neanderthal brain was significantly larger than the brains of modern humans.

A Typically Human Quality

The Neanderthals were the first creatures dignified by science with the name *Homo sapiens*, implying that they had most of the characteristics of modern human beings. Aside from their essentially modern physical make-up, this designation is largely based on the fact that they were the first people to consistently bury their dead. These burials, in at least one case accompanied by what appears to have been a large offering

Traditional Blood scaffold burial, southern Alberta.

of flowers, have great implications for how we view the intellectual development of these ancient creatures. During the hundreds of thousands of years prior to the Neanderthals, ancestral humans had learned to make stone tools, to control fire and to live in social bands or packs capable of hunting large animals and storing food for seasons of scarcity. But archaeological evidence cannot reveal what they thought of their world and of their place in it, or even whether they had an efficient means of communicating their thoughts to one another. We can infer much more about our ancient human ancestors after the Neanderthals began burying their dead. Firstly, we know that they had

adopted the essentially human belief that life continues in some form after death; their burials were meant either to help the souls of the deceased or to hinder ghosts that could harm the living. Secondly, they obviously had a form of communication approximately as efficient as modern language, which allowed them to share this belief, both within the local band and with other bands inhabiting much of Eurasia.

When the first ancestral Indians crossed Beringia into the New World, they brought with them a philosophy of life and death that can be at least vaguely reconstructed from the

The Great Serpent burial mound, in southern Ohio (right), measures over 400 metres from head to tail. This or similar mounds in the upper Mississippi Valley may have been the model for the Serpent Mound on Rice Lake (above).

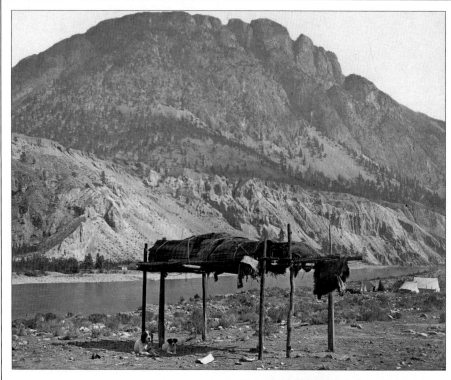

Haida grave-box on carved poles, Queen Charlotte Islands, British Columbia.

treatment of their dead. Throughout the late Palaeolithic period, human corpses were placed in the ground with some degree of ceremony and were often accompanied by tools or food apparently meant to help the soul of the deceased person in an afterlife. The dead were obviously thought to have entered another realm of life, either as revered ancestors from whom the living could expect help or as malevolent ghosts who had to be appeased. By about 5 000 years ago in the Old World, such ideas had been elaborated to produce the mummification and pyramid burials of Egyptian royalty and the massive megalithic tombs of Europe. The next 2 000 years produced many of the most elaborate burials of antiquity: the Royal Tombs at Ur in Mesopotamia, and the early Shang tombs of China, where a ruler was accompanied by horses and numerous retainers.

Parallel Evolution

The elaboration of burial rites among New World peoples kept pace with, and in some cases surpassed, those of the Old World. As we have seen, the 7 000-year-old mound buri- al of an adolescent at L'Anse-Amour on the Labrador coast is at least as complex as any burial known at that time. For the following 5 000 years the peoples of Atlantic Canada and the adjacent eastern woodlands maintained an impressive tradition of burial in local cemeteries: the bodies were covered with red ochre and accompanied by large numbers of grave-goods, including exotic items such as sea shells and native copper obtained by trade from distant sources. Elsewhere across the country, burials became more varied; occasional cremations or the absence of skeletons, suggesting some other form of disposal, indicate the development of local traditions.

Sometime after 1000 B.C., probably influenced by practices emanating from the Ohio and upper Mississippi valleys, the people of eastern Canada began to adopt new burial methods. The earliest of these burials, scattered from Ontario eastward to New Brunswick, are in low earth mounds containing specific grave-goods imported directly from the Ohio Valley. These burials are so similar to contemporaneous burials of the Adena people in the American Midwest that archaeologists have speculated that Adena missionary-traders roamed the eastern forests. During the first millennium A.D., when the Serpent Mound was built, influences from the south were still strong, but the burials do not reflect such a close connection to the people of the Ohio Valley.

Jean de Brébeuf's Account

Eighteenth-century engraving of the Huron Feast of the Dead. The artist worked from accounts written by Jesuit missionaries a century earlier, and had no direct knowledge of Huron life and traditions.

Twelve years or thereabout having elapsed, the Old Men and Notables of the Country assemble, to deliberate in a definite way on the time at which the feast shall be held to the satisfaction of the whole Country and of the foreign Nations that may be invited to it. The decision having been made, as all the bodies are to be transported to the Village where is the common grave, each family sees to its dead, but with a care and affection that cannot be described: if they have dead relatives in any part of the Country, they spare no trouble to go for them; they take them from the Cemeteries, bear them on their shoulders, and cover them with the finest robes they have. In each Village they choose a fair day, and proceed to the Cemetery, where those called *Aiheonde*, who take care of the graves, draw the bodies from the tombs in the presence of the relatives, who renew their tears and feel afresh the grief they had on the day of the funeral. I was present at the spectacle, and willingly invited to it all our servants; for I do not think one could see in the world a more vivid picture or more perfect representation of what man is. It is true that in France our cemeteries preach powerfully, and that all those bones piled up one upon another without discrimination, — those of the poor with those of the rich, those of the mean with those of the great, — are so many voices continually proclaiming to us the thought of death, the vanity of the things of this world, and contempt for the present life: but it seems to me that what our Savages do on this occasion touches us still more, and makes us see more closely and apprehend more sensibly our wretched state. For, after having opened the graves, they display before you all these Corpses, on the spot, and they leave them thus exposed long enough for the spectators to learn at their leisure, and once for all, what they will be some day.

*Coast Salish grave-house,
Vancouver Island*

At the time of European contact, the native peoples of Canada had developed a wide variety of burial traditions. In some societies there were multiple traditions, each applying to a certain segment of the community. Among some West Coast peoples, for example, nobles were buried in large wooden boxes placed atop mortuary poles; commoners were buried in the ground or placed in caves near the community, while the corpses of slaves were disposed of in the village shell midden or in the sea. Cremation was practised in some regions of British Columbia and in the northwestern forests. Across the Prairies, corpses were generally placed on scaffolds or in trees. The Algonquian peoples of the eastern forests used tree burial, at least during the winter when the ground was frozen, but also buried their dead in the earth or in caves. In the Arctic, where the earth is permanently frozen, Inuit corpses were buried beneath boulder cairns or left on the sea ice.

The Feast of the Dead

The most complex native Canadian burial ceremony on record is that of the Hurons of central Ontario, described by the seventeenth-century French missionaries. The Huron dead had been placed on wooden platforms in the trees of a cemetery close to the village, where their spirits would be close to the people left behind. But a Huron village was a temporary community, abandoned and reestablished elsewhere after 10 to 15 years, when the local firewood and soil fertility were exhausted. At the time the Hurons abandoned a village, they held an elaborate ceremony, which became known to the French as the "Feast of the Dead". They prepared for the ceremony by sending invitations to other villages and collecting large quantities of gifts. When the visitors arrived, a ten-day ceremony was held in honour of the dead, with games, gift-giving, feasting and dancing. The corpses were removed from the local cemetery, and the bones were cleaned of flesh by female relatives of the deceased. Visitors brought the bones of village people who had died in distant villages. Finally, an ossuary pit three metres deep and five or more metres across was dug near the village, and lined with beaver pelts and kettles. The bundles of bones that had been collected from the cemetery were ceremoniously deposited into the pit, where men with poles mixed them together as a symbol that the Huron individual, in death as in life, was most importantly a member of his community. A mound of earth and a wooden roof were then constructed over the pit. This ceremony released the souls of the dead, who until then had remained close to and protective of the village, and allowed them to journey westwards to a large village of their own.

The three small ossuary burial pits found near the Serpent Mound suggest that the site retained a sacred character for up to 1 000 years. The difference between these and the earlier mound burials indicates the extent to which the society changed its burial customs over a period of a millennium.

Far to the south, the first great civilizations of Meso-America were developing. At about this time, a large ceremonial centre was being built in the Mexican highlands, at the emerging city of Teotihuacan, which then covered an area of over 10 square kilometres. One of the most impressive constructions under way was that of the Pyramid of the Sun, a huge structure 64 metres high and 210 metres square at the base. Far to the north, in the valleys of the Mississippi and Ohio rivers, religious ideas from the south seem to have influenced the development of what archaeologists know as the Hopewell culture. We know the Hopewell people primarily from their burial mounds, which indicate a sophisticated religion with elaborate burial rituals. It has been suggested that these rituals were overseen by an elite priesthood who may also have directed the expansion of trade in order to obtain exotic materials for use as grave-goods. Probably through such trade contacts, elements of the Hopewell religion spread as far west as Kansas and as far north as Ontario. Burial mounds vaguely resembling those of the Hopewell people are scattered across southern Ontario and along the Rainy River drainage between Lake Superior and Manitoba.

The people who built the Serpent Mound had probably used the site as a summer mussel-collecting camp for several generations before selecting it as a burial location. For at least 4 000 years their ancestors had buried their dead with exotic grave-goods, probably with great ceremony, but had been content with single interments in selected cemetery areas. About 2 000 years ago, however, the occupants of the Rice Lake area began to build earthen mounds over the remains of their dead relatives. They had probably heard vague rumours of the large mounds built by the people of the Hopewell culture south of the lakes. Perhaps a traveller from the south had passed through the area on a journey of trade or exploration and had told the local people something of the religious ideas behind the Hopewell burial mounds. Or perhaps a party of local men had returned from the south, having seen the sophisticated Hopewell towns, and determined to emulate the religious practices of a culture that could produce such wealth.

By whatever means the burial-mound concept reached southern Ontario, it seems to have been received enthusiastically by several groups. The localities selected for construction may have been traditional burial grounds or areas thought to be sacred for other reasons. The wild rice and the mussel beds on the north shore of Rice Lake provided a food resource capable of supporting a gathering of local people for a few weeks each summer, and this resource may have influenced the selection of the site for the construction of mounds. Although we do not know which of the mounds were built first, we may guess that the Serpent Mound was a later embellishment, perhaps an imitation of the great serpent mound in what is now Adams County, Ohio.

The archaeological excavations carried out by the Royal Ontario Museum reveal burials both in the earth beneath the mound and in the mound fill itself. This suggests that construction occurred intermittently over a period of several years and that many burials had occurred as the work progressed. The large number of burials recovered – over 75 from the half of the Serpent Mound that was excavated and over 50 from the other mounds, plus an unknown number of skeletons removed by earlier looters – indicates that many generations of the local population were buried here.

An Unfinished Structure

The blunt eastern end of Serpent Mound has an unfinished look. Construction was stopped at some time in the first few centuries A.D., as it was, too, in the large Hopewell centres of the Ohio Valley. For some reason the influence of the Hopewell priesthood and its religion declined, and elaborate ritual burials decreased throughout northeastern North America. The Serpent Mound locality must have retained some significance to the local people, however, for the archaeologists have discovered that about 1 000 years later three ossuary burial pits were constructed close to the mounds. A few potsherds scattered through the upper levels of the site are witness to occasional visits to the area by Iroquoian people of the late Prehistoric period. By the time of these visits the original significance of the mounds must have been long forgotten, but the sacred character of the site may have been maintained in local traditions for well over a thousand years.

CHAPTER 8

INVADERS FROM THE NORTH

About A.D. 700 a massive volcanic eruption on the Alaska-Yukon border spread volcanic ash over an area of 250 000 square kilometres. If this event led to the dispersal of local Dene Indian groups, some of them may have undertaken one of the longest human migrations on record.

Bone arrowhead from a northern Dene archaeological site. This type of arrowhead was used primarily for hunting caribou.

Prehistoric archaeology generally functions within a time frame of centuries; our net of methods and techniques is simply too coarse-meshed to trap smaller periods of time. Rarely can we detect an event that occurred in a single day – or even a single year – and speculate on how this event may have influenced human history. One such event occurred in northwestern Canada about 1 300 years ago. As a background to examining this event, let us look briefly at three phenomena separated by half a world and more than a thousand years.

An Extraordinary Event

On 24 August, A.D. 79, Mount Vesuvius in southern Italy began to erupt. By the end of the following day the neighbouring towns of Pompeii and Herculaneum were buried beneath several metres of volcanic cinders and ash, and several thousand people had died. Archaeological excavation of these Roman towns has yielded our most dramatic information on what volcanoes can do to the populations living in their shadow, yet the eruption of Vesuvius apparently had very little effect outside a small local area. Other Mediterranean volcanoes have probably done much more to shape the history of the region. About 1500 B.C., a massive eruption destroyed the island of Santorini, and it now seems possible that the attendant earthquakes and tidal waves marked the end of the Minoan civilization centred on Crete, 100 kilometres to the south. It has even been suggested that Plato's story of Atlantis, a great island civilization suddenly destroyed by floods and earthquakes, may be related to the destruction of Minoan Crete by the Santorini eruption. Whether or not the identification is correct, it is clear that volcanic activity was capable of drastically affecting the course of prehistoric civilizations.

A Language of Northern Origin

The barren polychrome deserts of northern New Mexico and Arizona are the homeland of the Navaho, who, with a population of over 100 000, are by far the largest Indian nation in the United States. Traditionally a hunting people who for the past few centuries have been sheepherders and small farmers, the Navaho have worked out a practical compromise between the conditions of modern life in the American Southwest and their traditional beliefs and ways of life.

One of the most important traditional elements maintained by the Navaho is their language. Like that of the related Apache of the southern plains, the Navaho language bears no relationship to the languages spoken by other Indian groups of the area. Rather, it is closely related to the Dene (Athapaskan) languages spoken by Indians across northwestern Canada and Alaska, from Hudson Bay almost to Bering Strait, with offshoots extending southward into the interior plateau of British Columbia.

The Dene languages are very distinctive, apparently unrelated to any other American Indian tongues. During the Second World War, many Navaho served as radio operators with the United States Navy and Marines in the Pacific, and provided effective coded communications that mystified the Japanese.

The Dene languages were probably brought from Siberia by groups crossing to North America around the end of the last ice age when most of the continent was already occupied. The Dene took up occupation of the northwestern forests and probably expanded gradually throughout the region as they adapted their way of life to its resources, becoming a specialized northern-forest hunting people.

How, then, do we explain the isolated presence of Dene-speaking groups in the desert Southwest, living in an environment that could hardly be more different from that of their northern relatives, and separated from them by thousands of kilometres of country occupied by non-Dene groups? Linguists have long noted the remarkable similarity between the northern and southern Dene languages, and have suggested that the two groups parted company relatively recently. Using the techniques of glottochronology, which are based on questionable assumptions about the rates at which languages change, they suggest that the ancestors of the Navaho and Apache became isolated from other Dene groups only about 1 200 years ago. If we wish to understand why these people left their northern forest homeland for the southern desert, we may be wise to begin by looking at what was happening 1 200 years ago in northwestern Canada.

St. Elias range, western Yukon. The volcanic eruption that spread the White River Ash occurred in these mountains.

A Layer of Ash

A striking feature of riverbanks and road cuts throughout the southern Yukon and adjacent areas of British Columbia and the Northwest Territories is a horizontal band of white material stratified between beds of the usual brownish soil. The white material is volcanic ash; it is known to geologists as the White River Ash and can be traced to a massive volcanic eruption that occurred just west of the Alaskan border in the St. Elias Mountains. The ashfall extends approximately 1 000 kilometres eastward from its point of origin and covers an area of 250 000 square kilometres; near its origin, the fall was up to 1.5 metres deep. Recently obtained radiocarbon dates indicate that the eruption and consequent ashfall occurred around 1 250 years ago.

The possible historical significance of the White River Ash has recently been pointed out by William Workman, an archaeologist at the University of Alaska in Anchorage. His interest in the effect of volcanic events on the sparse aboriginal populations of northern North America grew from his archaeological work in the southern Yukon. At several of the sites he excavated, the White River Ash appeared as a prominent marker interrupting the sequence of archaeological remains left by the prehistoric occupants, probably ancestral Dene groups. What, he wondered, would such an ashfall have done to the local environment, and how would aboriginal peoples have coped with these changes? He began to study historical records of more-recent eruptions in Alaska and elsewhere. Most of these eruptions were much smaller than the one that deposited the White River Ash, but they caused massive environmental damage. To an isolated population of northern hunters, such events must have been terrifying, if not deadly.

We can only try to imagine what it must have been like to experience the White River ashfall. Around A.D. 700, the Yukon must have looked very much as it does today, and life for the few thousand Indian occupants of the area must have been quite similar to that of their nineteenth-century descendants before the Klondike Gold Rush changed their homeland forever. For most of the year they would have lived in small bands consisting of a few related families, in sporadic contact with similar groups among whom they had relatives or acquaintances. Those groups with access to salmon rivers would have depended heavily on this resource, and several bands would have come together to exploit the summer fishery. In the autumn, the larger groups would have broken up as individual families moved away to isolated winter camps from which the men could hunt caribou, moose and mountain sheep. The snow, cold, isolation and long nights of winter would often have brought hardship and privation. Geologists suggest that the accumulation of White River Ash on steep hillsides indicates that it fell with snow during winter, rather than with summer rain, which would have washed the ash from the slopes. It was, therefore, during winter, the hardest time of the year for the local people, that the volcanic eruption occurred.

A Dull Boom

It is unlikely that any families were in the high ranges of the St. Elias Mountains at that time of year to see the eruption. In the Yukon valleys, the first intimation of what was to come was probably a dull boom (easily mistaken for the settling of thick ice on a northern river) as an estimated 25 cubic kilometres of rock was blown into the sky as lava, pumice and fine ash. Some may have remembered the brief noise several hours later when the dogs began to howl and when sudden gusts of wind, the forerunners of the violent storms accompanying volcanic clouds, began to tear at the spruce trees around the sheltered tent camps. A man returning from checking on the dogs would report that snow had begun to fall and that there was a bad smell in the air. The tent would be warm and quiet, buried beneath the heavy snowfall, when the electrical storm began. Rare in summer and unknown in winter, the intense lightning and massive thunder must have provoked the terror that was to rule people's lives for the following days. Poorly understood stories of thunderbirds had probably reached the area from neighbouring peoples on the Pacific coast, and a winter thunderstorm could only have suggested the presence of powerful and unhappy beings. Proof could have come when a container of snow, brought indoors to melt for drinking water, was found to contain a foul-smelling liquid more gritty and silty than water from a glacial stream. Worst of all must have been the darkness, blacker than the most overcast night, while the foul snow fell.

When a smoky dawn finally broke, it must have revealed a world waist-deep or more in gritty greyish snow. Nevertheless, the rest of the winter was probably passed in relative ease. Fresh water and fish could be obtained from holes in

continued page 93

Digging
for
History

The question most commonly asked of archaeologists is how they know where to dig; yet, this is rarely a concern. In fact, most major archaeological sites have been discovered not by archaeologists but by local residents. The traditional stories of native communities often link historical events to specific locations. Farmers ploughing their fields or investigating unusual features on their land turn up many sites. Other archaeological sites are inadvertently uncovered by bulldozers working on pipelines, highways or subdivisions. For over a century, antiquaries and history buffs have made further discoveries as they explored their local areas. Finding a site is rarely a problem; it is usually more of a concern to salvage accidentally discovered remains before erosion or construction activity destroys them. Moreover, there are not enough

As archaeologists came to realize that information from the past lies in the ground itself and not just in artifacts removed from ancient sites, they began to develop techniques for recovering and recording this information. In this photograph of a mound excavation of the 1950s, the site has been mapped into a grid of squares and each square is being excavated as a unit. The walls between the squares serve as a record of the vertical stratigraphy. Digging with trowels and sweeping with brushes, the archaeologists are able to recover small objects and to record their location within each level of each square. Modern techniques of electronic mapping and recording now allow precise and accurate reconstructions of archaeological sites after they have been excavated.

trained archaeologists in the field to analyse archaeological discoveries before the sites are damaged.

A Sixth Sense

The training of archaeologists is quite different from the training of most other academic workers. The discipline is not really an art, for archaeologists must have a close knowledge of scientific method and of the processes known to the natural and human sciences. Yet it is not specifically a science, because each archaeological site is unique, and its interpretation is too complex to be reduced to a simple and testable set of procedures. It is probably best compared to a trade, such as carpentry or farming, in which academic training must be supplemented by a long apprenticeship. During this apprenticeship, the archaeologist learns how to dig and recognize the subtle distinctions between the various layers in the earth. What eventually emerges is a feel for what is in the ground, what it means and how it can be interpreted to yield a picture of life in the past.

An archaeological site is not simply a patch of earth containing a scatter of lost or broken artifacts. Rather, it is a mine of information, which can all too easily be lost or discarded. Some of this information is visible to the untrained eye if the excavation is carried out carefully enough. But most is revealed through stratigraphy, the study of how things came to be buried in the earth and later covered with other materials. For example, a small band of hunters may have camped on a lakeshore 10 000 years ago, leaving behind a stone-lined hearth and a few flint artifacts trodden into the beach sand. Later, the lake level may have dropped and the old shoreline became covered by forest, gradually burying the sand beneath a layer of humus soil. Perhaps 5 000 years later, a local community using this terrace as a cemetery dug through the humus and deep into the sand, and brought old flint tools to the surface of the forest soil. A thousand years ago an agricultural village may have become established nearby, its inhabitants using the edge of the terrace as a convenient place to dump their broken pottery and other garbage. Once the land had been cleared for farming, groundhogs excavated dens in the sandy soil, bringing to the surface a mixture of ancient flint tools, more-recent human bones and very recent pottery. Finally, a farmer may have dug a line of fence posts across the site, inadvertently helping the groundhogs in their work and bringing the site to the attention of archaeologists. In this example, the recognition and separation of ancient sandy beach soil, the soil of burial pits, and displaced soil produced by human and animal excavations is the art of stratigraphic excavation. Without this kind of basic analysis, the site would be only a curious mixture of artifacts and other information spanning a period of ten millennia.

Piecing Together the Past

Much of the information in an archaeological site is not directly visible. The textures of soils, and the microscopic particles contained in soils – plant pollen, parts of beetles, the bones of small, soil-living animals – allow a reconstruction of the environments in which the soils were produced. Such analysis could show that 10 000 years ago this particular site was on a lakeshore with sparse tundra vegetation and was frozen for most of the year; that the people who buried their dead here 5 000 years ago lived under a closed forest of massive pine trees; that the land was cleared for aboriginal farming 1 000 years ago, as indicated by a decline in tree pollen. Soil samples, carefully tied into the stratigraphic record, contain a great deal of information about the past.

Careless excavation can cause information to be lost by disturbing the distribution of artifacts on the site. Mapped and recorded, the scat-

Sir John W. Dawson
(1820-1899)

Naturalist, educator and geologist, Dawson was principal of McGill University for thirty-five years. He was responsible for the admission of women to the University. A founding member and president of the Royal Society of Canada, he was one of the first Canadian scientists of international renown.

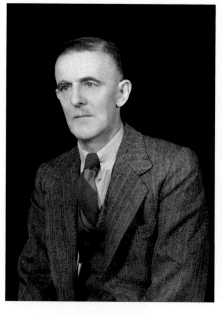

Diamond Jenness
(1886-1969)

On his first visit to the Canadian Arctic, 1913-15, Diamond Jenness acquired an interest in the Eskimo peoples which lasted throughout his life. The distinct cultures, "Dorset" and "Old Bering Sea" were defined by him.

ter of tools from an ancient hunting camp can reveal the size and arrangement of the tent, from which we might infer something about family organization. An analysis of the rings in the teeth of a caribou killed by these people can tell us that they occupied the site in the early spring, probably having followed the caribou migration from their homeland a few hundred kilometres to the south. Chemical analysis of the stone and copper tools found in burial pits might indicate that the people who buried their dead there 5 000 years ago had trade contacts ranging from Wyoming to Labrador.

Much information of this sort was lost from archaeological sites excavated in Canada during the last century, as it was from other major sites excavated around the world. The nineteenth century saw archaeology as a means of investigating the great questions that puzzled Europe in that era: Were humans a part of the animal world, rather than a special form of creation? Could biblical history be validated by the identification of the ancient cities and civilizations mentioned in Scripture? Were the legendary stories of classical Greece rooted in genuine historical fact? Such questions encouraged early antiquaries to dig into the ground, often with more enthusiasm than skill, and to bring home treasures that could fill early museums and support theories on the past.

The Precursors

The first Canadian archaeologists were also part of this movement to investigate man's place in nature. Sir Daniel Wilson of the University of Toronto excavated Huron sites, corresponded with Charles Darwin, and in 1862 wrote a book entitled *Prehistoric Man: Researches into the Origin of Civilization in the Old and New World*, which established him as an international figure in the study of early humanity. Sir John Dawson, a geologist who became principal of McGill University, developed an interest in the Iroquoian archaeology of Montréal, and in 1880 published *Fossil Men and Their Modern Representatives*, a significant contribution to nineteenth-century anthropology.

*Harlan I. Smith
(1872-1940)*

Smith joined the National Museum in 1911 to continue his study of the Archaeology of British Columbia. In the course of his long career, he undertook field work from coast to coast.

*W. J. Wintemberg
(1876-1941)*

Self-taught in the field of prehistory, Wintemberg worked with the National Museum from 1911 to 1940 and became an acknowledged expert on Ontario Iroquois.

Throughout the rest of Canada, most early archaeological work was undertaken by local antiquaries or by the wide-ranging geologists and natural scientists employed by the Geological Survey of Canada. Their collections eventually formed the basis for the National Museum of Canada. In the early twentieth century the National Museum began to hire staff archaeologists. Notable among them were Harlan I. Smith, who worked mainly on the West Coast; William J. Wintemberg, who carried out much of the early work from Ontario to Newfoundland; and Diamond Jenness, an ethnologist whose occasional but insightful archaeological contributions laid the foundation for our present knowledge of the prehistory of the North American Arctic.

Although the majority of Canadian archaeologists work at home, attempting to unravel the native and European history of this country, their endeavours have not been limited to the prehistory of Canada. An outstanding example is Davidson Black, a medical doctor working in China during the 1920s, who recog-

nized that some fossils being sold as medicines in Chinese drugstores were the teeth of primitive humans. This led to the identification of "Peking Man", the excavation of the very important site of Zhoukoudien near Beijing, and the eventual definition of *Homo erectus* as an ancestral form of human being. Canadians continue to contribute significantly to biblical archaeology in the Near East, to studies of the Palaeolithic hunters of Europe and to the reconstruction of the civilizations of both the Old and New worlds.

The second half of this century has seen an expansion of archaeology across Canada. All the provinces and territories have enacted laws dealing with the protection of archaeological sites and have established organizations designed to manage the archaeological resources of their regions. Most universities now offer training in archaeology, and societies of amateur archaeologists operate in most regions of the country. These societies usually fill the extremely useful role of auxiliary troops. Their training and talents can be called on in emergencies requiring quick action to salvage information that might otherwise be lost.

Protection of Sites

Despite the growth of archaeological bureaucracies, the discipline still depends largely on the goodwill and interest of an informed public: the farmer whose plough has turned up some ancient stone tools, and who agrees to delay planting a portion of a field until it can be investigated; the heavy-equipment operator who stops his engine when his blade uncovers an old copper kettle in a patch of red ochre, and his boss, who allows the archaeologists to excavate it before construction continues; or children who find arrowheads eroding on the banks of city ravines and bring them to the local museum. Each of these finds is a unique remnant of ancient human activity, another glimpse of a vanished way of life. If we miss too many such opportunities, much of the Canadian national heritage will be lost.

lake or river ice, while moose and caribou floundered in the deep snow that easily supported the snowshoes of the hunters. The immediate terror was past, but the real hardship was to come only with spring breakup. Although the country had been terribly polluted, most of the pollution still lay dormant, locked in the winter snowpack. When this snowpack began to melt, the spring runoff was saturated with chemicals and charged with fine ash. Fish populations were drastically reduced or wiped out, and no salmon could ascend the turbid rivers to spawn. Sheep and caribou, finding their summer food plants covered in ash, sickened and died as have domestic animals exposed to more-recent ashfalls, their teeth worn by ash and their joints swollen from ingested fluorine. The ash itself, scuffed into powdery clouds when dry and sucking grittily at moccasins when wet, made hunting or overland travel almost impossible.

A Critical Situation

Most of the small family groups probably survived the spring, living on porcupines, the inner bark of trees, and perhaps the occasional bear, grown fat from scavenging dead animals. Gathering at their traditional summer fishing places, they would have anxiously awaited the arrival of the salmon, the only resource that could now make their country habitable. As it gradually became apparent that the salmon were not going to come, it would have been equally apparent that the people could not remain. During the previous winter there must have been enough travel and visiting to have spread information on the extent of the ashfall – that, for example, three days' travel downriver to the north, or five days of packing through the ranges to the south, would bring them to an area where there was no ash. Some of these areas may have been uninhabited, but most were probably occupied by people who would have resented a large number of intruders. Families with relatives among these peoples were probably the first to leave the ash-covered areas; other families followed, hoping that their welcome would be smoothed by the earlier arrivals. As the situation became more desperate, others moved out in larger groups, prepared to bluff or fight their way to occupancy of a productive valley.

Although the ashfall probably resulted in relatively few human deaths, by the end of the first

Northern Dene woman and baby.

summer a large area of the Yukon must have been deserted, with several hundred refugees living in exile in the surrounding areas.

Archaeological evidence relating to these events is, as might be expected, very scarce; although the number of people affected might have been approximately the same as the population of Pompeii, these people were scattered over an area as large as Italy, an area still very poorly known archaeologically. We do know that the southern Yukon was reoccupied by people who used the same general styles of artifacts as those found beneath the ash. This reoccupation appears to represent a return of some of the previous occupants or their descendants, although we cannot tell whether it occurred within a decade or within a few centuries of the ashfall.

Refugees

In the northern Yukon, the ancestors of the Dene-speaking Kutchin arrived at about this time, using artifacts similar to those found beneath the ashfall to the south. It seems quite possible that these people were refugees who moved into an uninhabited area and established an occupation that has lasted to the present day. Farther south, on the interior plateau of British Columbia, the discovery of similar artifacts of the period

Nesjaja Hatali, Navaho Shaman from Arizona.

93

suggests the appearance there of ancestral Dene peoples. This region, however, was long inhabited by non-Dene Indians, and there must have been conflict between these established villagers and the small bands of wandering hunters from the north. Was this an intrusion by people who were simply searching for better hunting grounds, or by the descendants of northern refugees who had still not found a permanent home and were forced to risk their lives in other peoples' territories?

If the latter hypothesis is true, it could explain how the ancestors of the Navaho and Apache eventually arrived in the American Southwest. From the British Columbia Plateau, forested valleys with very similar environments stretch south as far as Utah and Colorado. While Dene hunters may have learned how to live in this environment, they may not have found a place where they could settle permanently. Few and weak compared to the peoples who had prior claim to the land, they may have been tolerated for years or even generations, as long as they lived in the back country and stayed out of the way. Eventually, however, they would inevitably be blamed for poor hunting or other misfortunes, and threatened or attacked until they moved on. Their wanderings may have come to an end only after several centuries, when they reached the desert Southwest, then occupied by village-dwelling farming groups. By occupying land that was useless for agriculture and by raiding the fields and storehouses of their farming neighbours, they could have begun to develop the hunting and raiding practices characteristic of the Navaho and Apache communities of the Historic period.

We cannot be sure that Workman is correct in linking the volcanic eruption resulting in the White River Ash with the dispersal of the Dene peoples. However, the timing of the two events is, to the best of our knowledge, so close that we may well suspect more than coincidence. An ashfall of this magnitude would have been one of the most harrowing natural experiences imaginable, and it could easily have produced human consequences as striking as the southern migration of the Navaho.

CHAPTER 9

ARCTIC WHALERS

The ancestors of the Inuit arrived in Arctic Canada only about 1 000 years ago. They were immigrants from Alaska who had developed a rich maritime hunting way of life, which they were able to adapt to the Canadian Arctic during the relatively mild Medieval Warm period. The colder climate of the past few centuries made their earlier way of life untenable, and led to the development of the classical Inuit culture of the Historic period.

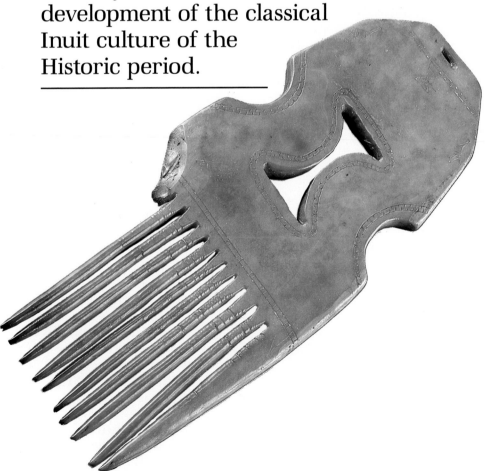

Woman's ivory comb found in a Thule winter house. The engraved decoration at the top of the handle includes a stylized representation of the flukes of a bowhead whale.

When nineteenth-century European explorers first began to penetrate the central Canadian Arctic, they found much of the country unoccupied. They occasionally met people on the southern islands and coasts, and returned to Europe with tales of fur-clad hunters barely surviving in a savage land. They were extremely impressed by the ingenuity that allowed such survival and in particular by the houses that sheltered these Inuit from winter cold – the domed snow houses (which have become known in English as igloos) built from blocks of hard-packed snow and heated by oil lamps.

Bering and Chukchi seas. This technology included bows of an Asiatic pattern, a wide variety of lances and darts propelled with a throwing board, harpoons and harpoon-float gear for the taking of sea mammals, and, perhaps most importantly, efficient boats. Two types of boats were used: the small hunting kayak and the umiak, a large skin-covered boat 10 metres or more in length and

Knives such as this, with a whale-bone handle and polished slate blade, were probably used by the Thule Inuit for flensing whales.

The Inuit snow house has captured the imagination not only of generations of schoolchildren, but also of scholars and architects. Constructed of an abundant local material, shaped so as to offer the least possible resistance to the winds of winter storms, and so well insulated that it can be heated by human bodies and the flame of a small lamp, the snow house has often been used as an example of a structure perfectly adapted to its environment.

capable of transporting an entire camp on rivers or along the coast. It was also from the umiak that these people, using large harpoon-float equipment, hunted the largest animal of northern waters, the bowhead whale. Whaling appears to have intensified along the coast of northern Alaska around A.D. 1000, and the people associated with this intensification are known to archaeologists as the Thule culture Inuit.

Before the Snow House

To an archaeologist, an attempt to trace the history of the snow house is rather frustrating – by virtue of its design, no other type of human structure leaves fewer traces. Some claim to have detected the remains of snow houses at sites up to 3 000 years old, on the basis of round patches of artifacts and refuse found with no surrounding rim of gravel or boulders that would have held down the edges of a tent. However, such features could also result from a circular tent pitched in winter snow.

We are fairly certain that the ancestors of the Inuit did not know how to build snow houses when they arrived in Arctic Canada about 1 000 years ago. These people came from Alaska, where for a thousand years or more they had developed the technology that enabled them to be very effective hunters of the rich coastal resources of the

Maritime Hunters

The Thule people specialized in open-water hunting of sea mammals and amassed great amounts of meat and blubber. Their ability to store food and fuel during the summer allowed them to live in relatively large and permanent coastal villages all winter. Along the coast of northern Alaska between Point Hope and Point Barrow, such communities were located at points where summer whaling was productive. Although the size of such communities is difficult to estimate, the nineteenth-century Inuit of the area continued to live an essentially Thule way of life in communities of up to 300 people occupying as many as 50 houses.

The dwellings of the Thule people of northern Alaska were variants of the Alaskan Eskimo pattern, differing primarily in their somewhat smaller size and the method of heating – by oil lamps rather than a central wood-burning hearth.

The houses were dug a metre or more into the earth, floors and walls were lined with driftwood, and the roofs were rafined with driftwood poles and covered with a thick layer of turf, into which was set a skylight made of gut. The entrance was a long turf-banked tunnel ending at a trapdoor in the floor. The rear half of the house was occupied by a wide wooden sleeping platform. Such houses were scattered randomly around the village area, and the entire settlement must have given the impression of a cluster of grass-covered mounds separated by ice cellars, drying racks, and the driftwood racks on which kayaks and umiaks were placed to protect them from the dogs.

The Thule Invasion

About 1 000 years ago, small groups of Thule people appear to have expanded eastwards along the coast of the Beaufort Sea and Amundsen Gulf in the western Canadian Arctic, the summering grounds of the bowhead whales that migrated along the northern coast of Alaska each spring. The remainder of Arctic Canada continued to be occupied by the Dorset people (known to archaeologists as the Palaeo-Eskimos), the descen-

dants of the first people to arrive in Arctic Canada, about 4 000 years ago. The Dorset people lacked much of the technology developed in Alaska during the previous millennium. They also seem to have had a much poorer way of life and much smaller communities. At some point, probably during the eleventh century A.D., this way of life was disrupted by an invasion of Alaskan Thule people. The Dorset culture thus disappeared from most of Arctic Canada.

The reason for the extremely rapid expansion of the Thule people across Arctic Canada and to Greenland cannot be accurately determined. One possible explanation is climatic change. The movement occurred during the Medieval Warm period, a few centuries during which agriculture

The winter houses of the Thule people were dug into the earth, lined with boulder walls and a flagstone floor, and featured a raised flagstone sleeping bench at the back. The roof was constructed of animal skins covered by an insulating layer of turf, supported by a framework of whale bones.

flourished in northern Europe (the limit of grape growing was far to the north of its present position), which may also have made possible the Norse occupation of Iceland, Greenland and other North Atlantic islands. Similar warm-weather conditions seem to have occurred in Arctic Canada, almost certainly resulting in a marked reduction in the extent and seasonal duration of sea ice and a subsequent increase in the population and range of the sea mammals upon which the Thule people depended. Thule villages across the High Arctic are studded with the bones of large whales, animals that today are found rarely if at all in these areas. It has been speculated that while moving north from the Amundsen Gulf to the Parry Channel, the Thule people may have discovered migrating herds of Greenland whales (the eastern Arctic equivalent of the bowhead) and followed them eastwards to their wintering grounds in Baffin Bay and the North Atlantic.

In Search of Metal

While the warm summers of this period obviously allowed the Thule people to expand an essentially Alaskan way of life across Arctic Canada, they may not actually have caused the expansion. This is suggested by the fact that the eastward movement did not occur during the previous two or three centuries, when the climate was as warm as during the eleventh century. Another factor influencing the expansion may have been a search for metal. The Alaskan Thule people and their ancestors had long since obtained small pieces of smelted iron from the Iron Age peoples of Siberia; these fragments supplemented their stone blades for weapons, knives and other tools.

The earliest Thule sites in the eastern Arctic are found not in the relatively rich southern portions of the Arctic Archipelago, but far to the north in the Thule District of northwestern Greenland (from which the culture takes its name) and the adjacent east coast of Ellesmere Island. In this area, a large fall of iron meteorites occurred at some undetermined time in the past. The iron was discovered by the late Dorset people during the few centuries immediately preceding A.D. 1000, and small pieces of meteoric iron

are found on Dorset sites of this period. Rumours of this new resource may have reached the Thule people of the western Arctic and sparked a rapid exploration and settlement of the eastern High Arctic. The earliest known Thule sites in the area contain metals from yet another source: smelted iron, copper and bronze from the Norse colonies established during the previous century in southwestern Greenland. Throughout the subsequent history of the Thule occupation of Arctic Canada, stone tools were almost totally replaced by small points and blades made from smelted metal, iron from the meteorites of Cape York in northwestern Greenland and native copper from the deposits in the Coppermine River region of the central Arctic.

Whale-Bone Houses

Whatever the explanation for the Thule expansion across Arctic Canada, these hunters found themselves in an environment quite different from that of their Alaskan ancestors. In most areas, sea mammal and caribou resources were adequate for the maintenance of permanent winter villages of the Alaskan type, though considerably smaller than those of the northern Alaskan coast. Although some archaeological sites of the Thule people of Canada contain the ruins of 30 or more winter houses, these probably represent occupation over a period of centuries; at any one time most or all of these villages consisted of perhaps only one to a dozen houses.

The Alaskan design of house construction persisted, with one notable difference: as most regions of Arctic Canada lacked the supplies of driftwood used to build Alaskan houses, the Canadian Thule people were forced to substitute local materials. They used materials much more durable than wood, so that the remains of their houses are much better preserved than are those of their Alaskan ancestors. The houses of the Canadian Thule, like those of their Alaskan ancestors, were

*This ivory handle from a Thule Inuit site
in the High Arctic is engraved with summer tents,
kayakers hunting caribou, two umiaks,
and men apparently shooting
at one another with bows.*

dug as much as a metre into the ground, and the earth walls were lined with boulders or slabs of rock instead of wood; the masonry was generally laid up to half a metre above ground level. In some villages, large whale bones or even skulls were used to supplement the boulders. The interior and entrance-passage floor of each house was flagged with neatly fitted stone slabs; similar slabs were raised on blocks to form the rear sleeping platform. Some of the slabs used in these houses are immense, requiring the strength of two or three men just to shift them. Such slabs must have been valuable commodities. (At a site that I excavated on Devon Island, broken slab fragments on a beach below the village suggest that they were brought by umiak from an outcrop 20 kilometres east of the village.) The roof of the house was supported by the mandibles of bowhead whales, strong and heavy bones up to five metres long, perhaps interlaced with whale ribs. This frame would first have been covered with heavy skins, then layered with turf gathered from nearby swales. When completed, the house would have been clean, strong, well insulated and practically airtight.

The ruins of hundreds of Thule winter villages dot the Arctic landscape: circles of boulder walls and collapsed roofs of whale bone; pits and boulder caches for the storage of food; sliding-door fox traps, and even polar-bear traps built of boulders and large slabs; stone-covered burials, cairns and other markers; and lines of slabs up to 90 metres long, used in a hopping game that was also a trial of strength. The Thule people seem to have delighted in moving and using large chunks of rock and whale bone; at one village on Devon Island the lintel over each house entrance was graced with the skull of a bowhead whale weighing several hundred kilograms. One archaeologist has referred to the Thule people's modification of the Arctic landscape as a geological event second only to the last continental glaciation. The sophistication of their construction was such that, when nineteenth-century British naval parties sent in search of the Sir John Franklin expedition encountered remains of Thule civilization in High Arctic areas unoccupied by Inuit, they mistakenly reported it as evidence of the lost expedition.

The Little Ice Age

What happened to the whale-bone houses and their occupants? This style of house seems to have been abandoned throughout the Canadian Arctic because of a cooling climate that set in after the thirteenth century and culminated in the Little Ice Age, from approximately 1550 to 1850.

continued page 106

Thule hunters return to a small winter village on an Arctic coast.

The Little Ice Age

Inuit travelling by umiak in Hudson Strait. Boats such as this were used for hunting and travelling in open water during the relatively warm summers of the Thule period.

One of the most marked changes in climate to affect the Northern Hemisphere occurred between approximately A.D. 1550 and 1850. During this period, known as the Little Ice Age, severe winter storms and bitterly cold weather were much more common than in the centuries before or since. Rivers and canals froze throughout northern Europe, and there were skating parties on the Thames in London. In Norway and Switzerland, mountain villages were overrun by advancing glaciers. Crops failed, and northern European vineyards were no longer productive. The Norse abandoned their colonies in Greenland, while their Icelandic relatives underwent great hardship and starvation. In the Chinese province of Kiangsi, the traditional cultivation of oranges was discontinued.

Studies of tree rings, pollen deposits and other natural phenomena indicate that this widespread cooling also affected Canada during the same period. Yet, while there were major changes in the traditional ways of life of many aboriginal Canadians, it is difficult to determine the

A train of dogsleds moves an early-twentieth-century Inuit community from one temporary winter village to the next on the sea ice of the central Arctic.

Inuit fishing for char at a stone weir in a river of the central Arctic. Interior fishing became increasingly important as summers became cooler and sea ice more extensive.

extent to which they were caused by the climatic changes. The Little Ice Age occurred at the same time as the major European exploration and exploitation of eastern Canada and the development of the fur trade in the north and the west. Much of the disruption of native ways of life was probably directly attributable to the impact of European diseases, and involvement in a European economy, rather than to climatic change. Yet, the unexpected severity of winter weather must have contributed to the problems faced by native peoples adapting to the newcomers who were spreading across their continent.

Only in the Far North, beyond the reach of direct European influence, did the Little Ice Age cause major cultural change. The ancestral Inuit abandoned the islands of the High Arctic and developed new ways of life that were less dependent on summer hunting in open water. Like Swiss farmers, French viticulturalists and Chinese orange growers, the Inuit were forced to make a major adjustment in their way of life in order to adapt to an unexpected change in climate. The Little Ice Age was a major factor in producing the distinctive Inuit cultures described by European explorers of the past few centuries.

*Slow and docile bowhead whales
can be approached and harpooned by hunters
paddling an umiak.*

Increased sea ice probably restricted the movement of whales into Arctic waters where they had previously been abundant and decreased the populations of other sea mammals upon which the Thule people had depended. The High Arctic north of the Parry Channel was abandoned, and throughout the Central Arctic the Inuit descendants of the Thule people began to depend more heavily on seals, caribou and fish. Unable to stock sufficient supplies for the winter season, they adopted a more mobile winter life that allowed them to subsist on small ringed seals, which could be hunted at their breathing holes. The new way of life created the need for a different type of dwelling, however, and the domed snow house was developed to meet this need.

In the long run, the whale-bone house proved poorly adapted to the conditions of human life in Arctic Canada. However, it should be appreciated as an example of ingenuity in the use of local materials, as well as for its contribution to the Arctic landscape. For more than 500 years such houses provided secure and comfortable shelter to an entire population and must have been an important element in the occupation of Arctic Canada by the ancestors of the Inuit.

CHAPTER 10

ARTISTS OF THE BADLANDS

The sandstone cliffs of the Milk River valley in southern Alberta are carved and painted with one of the largest collections of rock art in the world. Who were the artists, and what did they intend to portray?

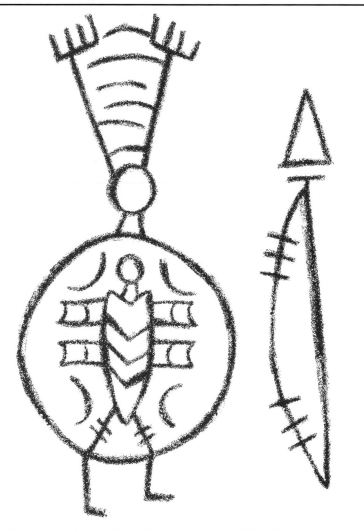

Warrior with bow and decorated shield, carved into the cliffs at Writing-On-Stone.

The plains of southern Alberta rise in a series of gentle waves toward the western mountains. At the place called Writing-On-Stone, a few kilometres east of the town of Coutts, the horizon is broken only by the Sweetgrass Hills across the nearby Montana border and by the deep gash of the Milk River as it arcs through Alberta before turning south to join the Missouri. The windswept plains support a sparse vegetation of bunchgrass, cactus and sagebrush, while clumps of cottonwoods grow in the narrow and protected valley bottom. In the past this was prime buffalo country.

Sacred Territory

In the area around Writing-On-Stone, the Milk River has cut downwards through the soft sandstone, so that its present bed lies as much as 50 metres below the surrounding country. The steep valley walls are lined with long stretches of sheer sandstone cliffs overlooking fields of hoodoos – strangely shaped sandstone columns capped and protected from erosion by boulders or slabs of harder rock. In contrast to the uniformity of the surrounding plains, the scenery is striking and bizarre. This is perhaps why the area has been considered sacred for centuries or even millennia by the various Indian groups who have lived in the region. The significance of the site is recorded in the history and legends of the Blackfoot and confirmed by the thousands of carved or painted glyphs that give the site its name.

The first white man to see the glyphs was James Doty, who visited "the Writings" in 1855. Describing the cliffs, he wrote: "They are worn by the action of the weather into a thousand fantastic shapes, presenting in places smooth perpendicular surfaces covered with crude hieroglyphics and representations of men, horses, guns, bows, shields etc., in the usual Indian style." The site has long been famous locally, and most of the glyphs are now within the boundary of Writing-On-Stone Provincial Park. In 1976 the Alberta Parks Department sponsored the first systematic inventory of the rock art. This work, which was carried out by James D. Keyser of the University of Tulsa, and the results of more recent archaeological excavations give us a reasonably complete picture of the history and significance of the site.

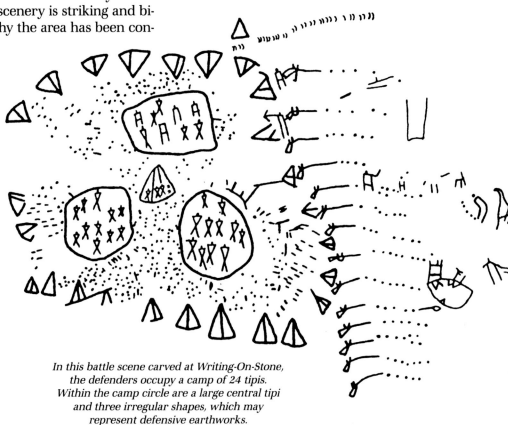

In this battle scene carved at Writing-On-Stone, the defenders occupy a camp of 24 tipis. Within the camp circle are a large central tipi and three irregular shapes, which may represent defensive earthworks.

The camp is defended by a line of 14 rifles, each spewing dots representing bullets.

Keyser and his team found 58 localities where rock art occurred; the features ranged from a single glyph to panels containing thousands of figures. Almost all had been pecked or scratched into the soft rock; the remainder had been painted with red ochre. It soon became apparent that there were two types of representation, which Keyser called Ceremonial Art and Biographical Art, suggesting that the former was the earlier of the two styles.

Ceremonial Glyphs

The glyphs assigned to the Ceremonial Art style are usually large and deeply incised figures of humans and animals. With over 300 examples, human figures are the most frequently represented motif, depicted in a distinctive V-neck style with upward-pointing shoulders. About one-quarter of the V-neck figures carry large circular shields that cover the body from neck to foot; most of the shields are fringed and painted with heraldic designs. Many of the figures are armed with bows, lances or clubs. Most of the depictions seem to be of single figures, and the only scenes showing action involve combat between individuals. Animals are also represented, gracefully stylized with crescentic bodies, "heart lines" between the mouth and the heart, and the distinguishing characteristics of elk, deer, mountain sheep, antelopes and even skunks.

The horse is depicted very rarely compared with its frequency of portrayal in the more recent pictographs at the site. Only seven of over 250 depictions of horses are ascribed to the Ceremonial Art style, and these are crude representations with awkwardly drawn riders. Horses, moving northwards from the Spanish colonies of the American Southwest, first reached the northwestern plains during the eighteenth century, and the artists of the Ceremonial Art style seem to have been only vaguely familiar with them or had seen them only at a distance. In two depictions, however, a horseman with a lance is shown attacking a shield bearer on foot, suggesting closer observation on at least a few occasions.

Who were these prehistoric artists drawing animals and unmounted shield-bearing warriors on the cliffs along the Milk River? Similar pictographs found to the south, in Montana and Wyoming, suggest a southern affiliation of the Ceremonial Art style. The artists were probably Shoshone Indians, ancestors of tribes that inhabited the Great Basin of the desert Southwest during the Historic period. These people are thought to have expanded northwards along the eastern flanks of the mountains as far as southern Alberta in about 1300. Their way of life must have been

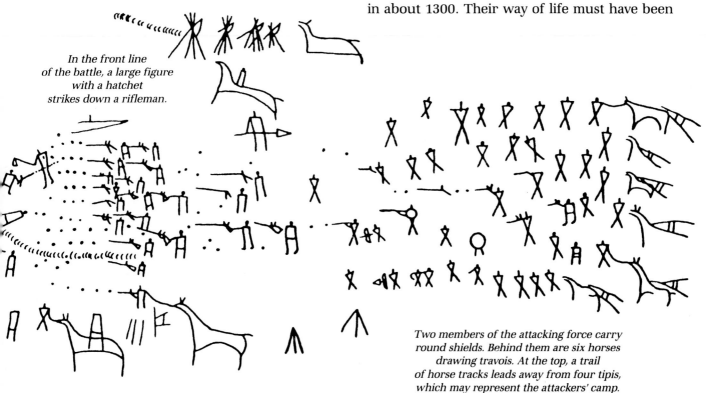

In the front line of the battle, a large figure with a hatchet strikes down a rifleman.

Two members of the attacking force carry round shields. Behind them are six horses drawing travois. At the top, a trail of horse tracks leads away from four tipis, which may represent the attackers' camp.

a variant of that practised on the northwestern plains for thousands of years, in which pounds or jumps were used for the hunting of bison. Communities probably consisted of small groups of related families, hunting and travelling on foot; they cannot have been as numerous or economically secure as the mounted bison hunters of the Historic period. Magical and ceremonial rites were probably practised as aids to both hunting and warfare, and at least one aspect of these religious activities may be the Ceremonial Art at Writing-On-Stone.

Biographical Art

The appearance of the horse not only transformed life on the northwestern plains; it also caused the disappearance of the shield-bearing warriors from southern Alberta. The next occupants of the area hunted and fought from horses and used the cliffs of Writing-On-Stone for a different type of art – the so-called Biographical Art style. The glyphs in this style are generally executed with less precision than those of the earlier period, often merely scratched into the soft rock. The large shields, probably too awkward to be useful in mounted warfare, are gone,

V-necked man with heart line, holding a rake-like or feathered object. Figures like this are characteristic of the Biographical Art style at Writing-on-Stone.

One of the more striking images of the Peterborough petroglyphs, near Stony Lake, Ontario, is this long-necked figure with a head that seems to represent the sun. It is surrounded by smaller representations of humans and animals.

as are the graceful representations of crescentic animals with heart lines. The emphasis now is on simple, almost stick-like human figures with rectangular or hourglass-shaped bodies, usually engaged in combat and often riding horses. Flying arrows are represented by dashes, and lines of dots symbolize bullets from guns, now portrayed for the first time. The fact that many of the same conventions can be found on the hide paintings of the Blackfoot and other Indians of the Historic period who populated the northwestern plains suggests that these peoples' ancestors were the creators of the Biographical Art at Writing-On-Stone.

The most impressive panels in this style show entire scenes apparently commemorating or recording actual events. A particularly complex scene, roughly three metres long, shows a battle involving 115 warriors: A camp circle of 24 tipis encloses three oval areas (interpreted as defensive earthworks), each containing a number of people; the outer edge of the camp is defended by a line of 14 flintlock rifles spewing bullets at the aggressors; the attacking force comprises 71 warriors, many armed with rifles, accompanied by a number of horses pulling travois; and in the centre of the scene two warriors are engaged in individual combat, in which a very large attacker strikes with a hatchet at a defending gunman. It is tempting to suggest that this attacker represents the artist of the panel, who is the first to make direct contact with the enemy, a major goal in Plains Indian warfare. Although there is no indication of the outcome of the battle, the numerical superiority of the attackers suggests that they may have been the victors and consequently the authors of the panel.

White Settlers Arrive

The intrusion of Europeans into the northwestern plains can be discerned in the glyphs, and not exclusively from representations of items such as swords and rifles acquired in trade. Another side of Indian-White relations is suggested by the brands on several horses in the pictographs; since the Plains Indians did not brand their horses, these animals had probably been

continued page 114

Sacred Places

The badlands of the Milk River valley – a gash in the rolling plains, filled with bizarre columns and naturally sculptured rock-forms – is a very impressive piece of landscape. Little imagination is required to interpret such an unusual locale as the home of spiritual beings. As much as 3 000 years ago, it may have been used as a site for vision quests or for vigils by shamans attempting to commune with the spiritual world. Some of the earliest rock carvings, now destroyed by erosion, may have recorded the results of such visits. The petroglyphs themselves must have enhanced the sacred character of the site, a character maintained in local tradition to the present day.

A Wealth of Sacred Sites

A few centuries ago, the land that is now Canada was filled with similar sacred places. Most have disappeared without trace, as a result of the suppression of native religious beliefs and the decreased use of native languages and place-names. The locations of a few such places are remembered in native religion, recorded by Europeans or marked by rock art like that at Writing-On-Stone. Most of these places are visually impressive, standing out from the local landscapes.

The religions of native Canadians peopled the world with spiritual beings, many of which lived beneath the earth or in the sky. Points where the underworld and the sky came into close contact with the surface of the everyday world held special significance as places where communication with the spirit world was possible: high hills, sheer cliffs, caves, underground streams, or waterfalls in which the voices of spirits could be heard. One such sacred place lies in the heart of Ottawa, just behind the Parliament Buildings: the set of rapids on the Ottawa River that the early French explorers called the Chaudière, the cauldron. A particularly powerful spirit lived beneath the bubbling white water, its voice audible in the rumbling roar of the rapids, and travellers left tobacco on a rock ledge to appease the spirit and ensure a safe journey.

The designation of sacred places was not unique to native Americans; it seems to be a widespread or even universal element of human cultures. The temples of ancient Greece were built on already-sacred places; the temples only provided a location in which to worship a god or spirit whose presence was attested by some feature of the natural landscape. The temple of Apollo at Delphi, perhaps the most important centre of the Greek religion, was located over a hole in a rock leading to a cave and underground stream, whose voice was interpreted by the oracular priestess to guide the affairs of state.

A Carved Panel

A sacred site with similar qualities, one apparently lost to tradition, was discovered in 1954 about 50 kilometres northeast of Peterborough in central Ontario. A party of prospectors who had settled down for a smoke break on a broad dome of limestone noticed that its white surface was marked by numerous shallow indentations. Stripping off the moss that covered much of the rock, they uncovered a large panel of carved forms representing thunderbirds, snakes, humans, boats and other images. Archaeological recording has now shown that this sheet of rock is covered with approximately 900 petroglyphs; a few stone tools and pottery sherds found on the site suggest that the petroglyphs were carved between approximately 500 and 1 000 years ago.

The site is isolated, distant from any large lake, stream or other travel route, and the reason for its selection as a sacred location is not apparent at first glance. Closer examination, however, suggests why this site was chosen for the execution of such a quantity of art. The smooth convex surface of white crystalline limestone seems out of place in this Canadian Shield country, dominated by jagged and hard igneous rocks. The limestone is relatively soft, and when the weathered surface is removed by pecking or

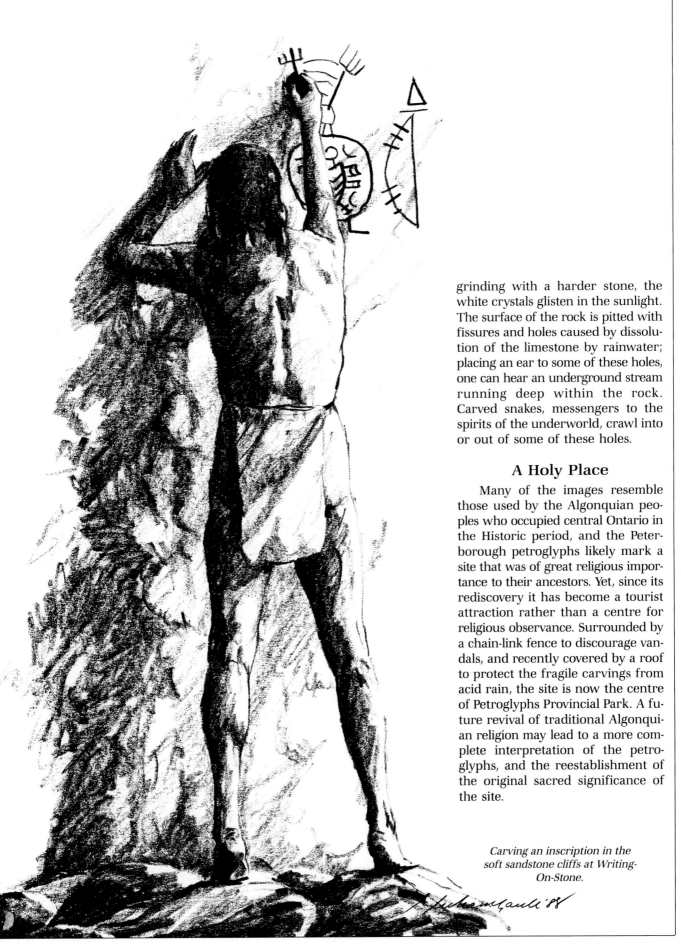

grinding with a harder stone, the white crystals glisten in the sunlight. The surface of the rock is pitted with fissures and holes caused by dissolution of the limestone by rainwater; placing an ear to some of these holes, one can hear an underground stream running deep within the rock. Carved snakes, messengers to the spirits of the underworld, crawl into or out of some of these holes.

A Holy Place

Many of the images resemble those used by the Algonquian peoples who occupied central Ontario in the Historic period, and the Peterborough petroglyphs likely mark a site that was of great religious importance to their ancestors. Yet, since its rediscovery it has become a tourist attraction rather than a centre for religious observance. Surrounded by a chain-link fence to discourage vandals, and recently covered by a roof to protect the fragile carvings from acid rain, the site is now the centre of Petroglyphs Provincial Park. A future revival of traditional Algonquian religion may lead to a more complete interpretation of the petroglyphs, and the reestablishment of the original sacred significance of the site.

Carving an inscription in the soft sandstone cliffs at Writing-On-Stone.

stolen from military posts or early ranches. The most explicit portrayal of Indian-White relations depicts two men hanging from gallows, one of which bears a flag; a horse-drawn wagon is driven by a man wearing cross-shaped headgear (a wide-brimmed hat?), a similar figure stands beside the wagon, and three rectangles with chimneys probably represent European-style buildings. The hanging seems to have occurred in a white fort or settlement, and the men on the gallows are probably Indians.

Just as the arrival of the horse over a century earlier marked the termination of the Ceremonial Art style, so the arrival of White settlers and the disappearance of the buffalo brought an end to the use of Writing-On-Stone as a site to record the battles and other exploits of the Indians of southern Alberta. Yet, although the last glyphs were probably carved around 1880, the site remains sacred in Blackfoot tradition.

According to this tradition, the glyphs at Writing-On-Stone were created not by humans, but by spirits. Apinaksinaks (who signed the 1877 Blackfoot Treaty) acquired his name, which means "Morning Writing", after courageously spending a night at the site and finding new inscriptions on one of the cliffs the next morning. Another man, who stayed overnight at Writing-On-Stone despite warnings from the spirits and who consequently died, reported that he saw inscriptions being carved by bluebirds.

This tradition of the supernatural origins of the depictions probably arose because the Blackfoot are relative newcomers to the area, having occupied southern Alberta for only two or three centuries. When they first reached the Milk River valley, they found the cliffs already covered with carvings – the shield-bearing warriors and crescentic animals carved and painted by the people who had lived in the area before them. Even during the Blackfoot occupancy, other tribes, such as Cree, Gros Ventre and Assiniboine, moved through the area, and each group may have added inscriptions without the knowledge of the others. The mysterious appearance of such inscriptions must have lent credence to the theory of supernatural origin.

A 3000-Year Tradition

The predecessors of the Blackfoot, the people who drew the shield-bearing warriors, are estimated to have moved into the area no earlier than about 1300. Did they, too, simply add their glyphs to panels already carved? No traces of earlier petroglyphs have been found, but this may be because of the rapid erosion of the very soft sandstone. Archaeological work carried out in 1977 by Jack Brink of the Archaeological Survey of Alberta suggests that earlier glyphs may once have existed. Excavation of the ground beneath the petroglyph panels revealed a thin scatter of burnt bones from butchered animals, flint flakes and occasional artifacts, including chipped-flint lance points fashioned in styles employed up to 3 000 years ago. Some of the finds were buried as much as a metre deep in sand eroded from the cliff face. Despite the evidence of long-term use of the site, it is interesting to note that no major camp was discovered. This is consistent with the historical evidence, which indicates that people did not camp at the site because of its sacred character, but visited it only occasionally to seek spiritual guidance from the inscriptions or to record visions, dreams and important events.

According to archaeological evidence, various groups of Indians have visited Writing-On-Stone for at least the past 3 000 years, and the sparseness of the remains suggests that the pattern of the earlier visits was similar to that of the Historic period. Deeper excavations may reveal even earlier use of the site. We do not know how many millennia have passed since the first individual hunter or group of travellers, struck by the bizarre setting of the site, commemorated the visit by inscribing pictures on the soft sandstone cliffs, thus starting a tradition of veneration of the site that has continued to the present time.

CHAPTER 11

THE PEOPLE OF HOCHELAGA

Just to the south of Montréal's Sherbrooke Street, construction excavations have for over a century turned up artifacts from a prehistoric settlement. Are these the remains of the town of Hochelaga, visited by Jacques Cartier in 1535?

Cooking pot, decorated like those of the St. Lawrence Iroquois around the time of Jacques Cartier.

Downtown Montréal – a huddle of high-rise buildings and paved parking lots squeezed between Mount Royal and the St. Lawrence River – is not the most promising environment for prehistoric archaeology. Yet somewhere beneath the walls and sidewalks lie the remains of a town whose name most of us remember from grade-school history classes. On 2 October 1535, Jacques Cartier reached the farthest point of his journey up the St. Lawrence River. Leaving his boats at a point on the shore where he was met by a crowd of over 1 000 people, he and his companions were led along a road through an oak forest toward the town of Hochelaga. After about five kilometres they were met by one of the town's headmen, who delivered a speech of welcome. Continuing, they found themselves walking through extensive cornfields, in the midst of which, under the brow of the hill they would later climb and name Mount Royal, they came upon a town such as no European had ever seen.

A Fortified Town

According to Cartier's description, the town was surrounded by a circular palisade built of logs. Within the palisade were some 50 houses, each over 50 paces long and 12 to 15 paces wide, built of wooden poles and covered with large sheets of bark. In contrast to the single-family housing of sixteenth-century France, these were communal houses, each occupied by an entire lineage of families. After a day of complex rituals, which always seem to occur when alien civiliza-

Smoking-pipe in the form of a human figure. The small size and unique design of this pipe suggest that it may have been fashioned by a youth.

tions come into contact for the first time, Cartier's small band of sailors was led to the top of Mount Royal, told of the geography of the country and escorted back to their boats.

After that day, Hochelaga and its inhabitants disappeared from the historical records. Six years later, on his third and final voyage, Cartier passed close to what was probably the same town, but he now referred to it as Tutonaguy. Scholars have speculated that in the intervening period Cartier had learned the real name of the community and that the name Hochelaga referred to a region and not its chief town. When Champlain reached the area in 1603, he found no town and a totally uninhabited Montréal Island. The more recent occupants of the island were Algonquians, who seem to have moved into the area from the north during the seventeenth century. The disappearance of Hochelaga is one of the small mysteries of Canadian history.

A century after Cartier's final voyage, the town of Montréal was founded. For its first two centuries the town remained close to the river, so that by the middle of the nineteenth century much of the land bordering Mount Royal was still under cultivation. During the latter part of the century, however, the city expanded rapidly to the very slopes of the mountain. In the course of this expansion, Hochelaga once again became the subject of scholarly debate and public interest. In 1860, workmen excavating sand (for use in construction) from a knoll in a field just south of Sherbrooke Street found the remains of human burials. For some time, they reburied them in the clay underlying the sand they were removing. Eventually, however, word of the discoveries came to the attention of Sir John W. Dawson of nearby McGill University. A man with wide interests in both natural and human history, Dawson was given a collection of skulls and artifacts gathered by the workmen and began visiting the site to collect further material.

The Site of an Old Settlement

Dawson found that the area under excavation was not just an ancient cemetery, but the site of a settlement. Patches of ash and charcoal marked the locations of hundreds of cooking fires; dark stains in the sand indicated the locations of wooden posts that had decayed in the ground, where houses had stood; and garbage dumps up to a metre deep contained charcoal, animal bones,

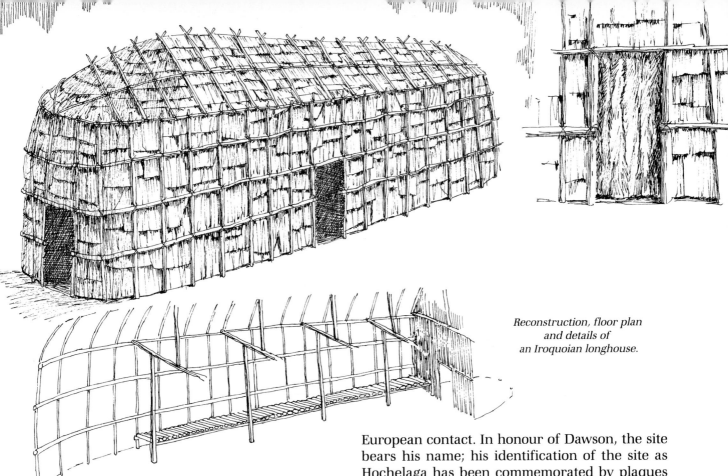

Reconstruction, floor plan
and details of
an Iroquoian longhouse.

plant remains, broken pottery and other objects. To an archaeologist accustomed to describing the location of a site with regard to local natural topography, Dawson's description seems rather incongruous. The finds, he wrote, "occur abundantly on the S.W. side of Metcalfe street, on the margin of the little brook which separates this site from the similar platform on which the building for the ball in honour of the Prince of Wales was erected, and they extend thence to Mansfield street, and from the margin of the terrace toward St. Catherine street more than halfway to Sherbrooke street, or in all a space of rather more than 1,200 yards in diameter." This was true urban archaeology and, like most work of this kind, was essentially a salvage operation; by the following year the site was entirely cleared of its sand layer. All that is left from the original site are the collections hurriedly made by Dawson and others, which are now preserved in several museums in Montréal and elsewhere.

Dawson was the first to suggest that the site was the remains of Cartier's Hochelaga. He based his identification on Cartier's description of the village's location and on the discovery at the site of a few small pieces of smelted metal, indicating

European contact. In honour of Dawson, the site bears his name; his identification of the site as Hochelaga has been commemorated by plaques for over a century. One of these still stands on the McGill University campus across the road from the site on Sherbrooke Street. The debate over whether or not the Dawson site was Hochelaga has created a small-scale academic industry among historians in the Montréal area. They have used a wide variety of evidence, ranging from linguistics to the topography and stream patterns of ancient Montréal, to support or deny the identification. The definitive book on the subject, *Cartier's Hochelaga and the Dawson Site*, was published a decade ago by Bruce Trigger, one of Canada's foremost prehistorians, and James Pendergast, an amateur archaeologist who has long specialized in the prehistory of the upper St. Lawrence valley. The book gives a good insight into the type of detective work involved in the practice of archaeology, especially when problems are difficult to solve because there is simply too little evidence available.

Iroquoian Tradition

What evidence supports the identification of the Dawson site as the remains of Hochelaga? First, Cartier recorded a basic vocabulary of the language spoken by the people of Stadacona, the first village he visited near Québec. Since the Stadaconans and the Hochelagans were related

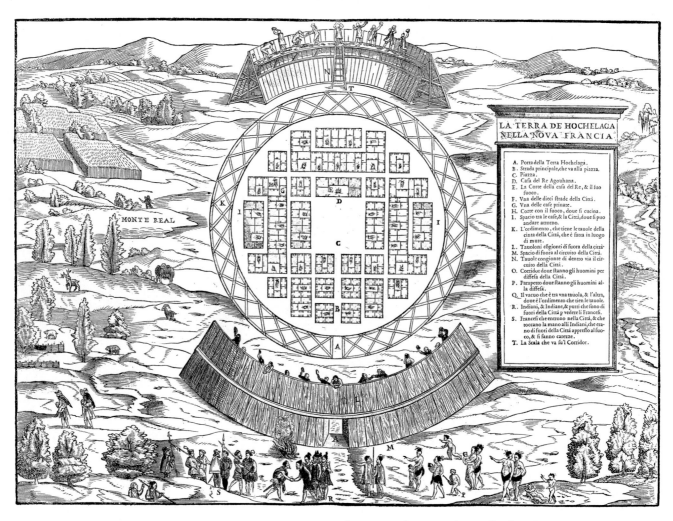

LA TERRA DE HOCHELAGA
NELLA NOVA FRANCIA

A. Porta della Terra Hochelaga.
B. Strada principale, che va alla piazza.
C. Piazza.
D. Casa del Re Agouhanna.
E. La Corte della casa del Re, & il suo
     fuoco.
F. Vna delle dieci strade della Città.
G. Vna delle case priuate.
H. Corte con il fuoco, doue si cucina.
I. Spacio tra le case, & la Città, doue si puo
     andare attorno.
K. L'ordimento, che tiene le tauole della
     cinta della Città, che è fatta in luogo
     di mure.
L. Tauoloni cõgionti di fuora della città.
M. Spacio di fuora al circuito della Città.
N. Tauole congionte di dentro via il cir-
     cuito della Città.
O. Corridor doue stanno gli huomini per
     diffesa della Città.
P. Parapetto doue stanno gli huomini al-
     la diffesa.
Q. Il vacuo che è tra vna tauola, & l'altra,
     doue è l'ordimento che tien le tauole.
R. Indiani, & Indiane, & putti che sono di
     fuori della Città p vedere li Francesi.
S. Francesi che entrano nella Città, & che
     toccano la mano alli Indiani, che era-
     no di fuori della Città appresso al fuo-
     co, & si fanno carezze.
T. La Scala che va su'l Corridor.

Jacques Cartier is welcomed to Hochelaga in this imaginative sixteenth-century drawing.

groups, it is assumed that the same language was spoken by both. The vocabulary is related to languages spoken by the Iroquoian peoples of Ontario and New York State. The pottery and other materials collected by Dawson are in the Iroquoian cultural tradition, but are distinct from those produced by other contemporaneous Iroquoian peoples. Cartier's description of Hochelaga fits that of an Iroquoian farming town, and Dawson collected the remains of maize, beans and wild plants, as well as the bones of animals and fish. Radiocarbon dating of the material collected by Dawson tells us only that the site was probably occupied within a century of Cartier's visit, as the technique is incapable of greater precision. More precise is Pendergast's analysis of the pottery and tobacco pipes fabricated by the inhabitants of the site. This analysis indicates that the Dawson site is the latest known prehistoric site in the area, dating probably to the time of European contact. Of special importance are the nine small pieces of smelted metal in the collections: a small bead of sheet brass, another scrap of brass and several small chunks of iron. If these objects actually originated from the Iroquoian occupation of the site and not from more recent levels, they would be consistent with the small amount of European trade material that probably reached the area during the early sixteenth century.

However, evidence is also set forth against the identification of the site as Hochelaga. First, it is pointed out that the site appears too small to be the settlement described by Cartier. From his accounts, Hochelaga (or Tutonaguy, if that was its actual name) is estimated to have had a population of 1 500 – not unusual for an Iroquoian town. Such a settlement must have been considerably larger than the area described by Dawson. Yet much of the site may have disappeared before being seen by Dawson; by his account, the workmen had destroyed much richer deposits than those remaining when he learned of the site. Over the years, Trigger and other archaeologists have kept an eye on construction trenches in the area, but have found no evidence that the site was larger than originally reported. Quite simply, the site probably disappeared in the nineteenth century.

continued page 122

Ancient Pottery

The discovery that lumps of common clay could be baked by fire into a material resembling stone seems to have been made at several different times and in several different places around the world. The first pottery was produced in Japan as early as 10 000 years ago; it appeared in the Middle East about 8 000 years ago, and in South America at least 5 000 years ago. Pottery was a very useful invention, especially for people who lived on seeds, grains and other vegetable foods that required dry, rodent-proof storage and considerable processing before they could be eaten. Unlike containers made of basketry, bark, hide or wood, ceramic pots could be used directly over a fire, thereby greatly increasing the efficiency and variety of cooking techniques.

The earliest pottery in Canada was invented or introduced in the Lower Great Lakes area sometime between 1000 and 500 B.C. Before the time of European contact, ceramic storage and cooking pots were produced in vast numbers by the agricultural Iroquoian peoples of this region. These pots ranged in size from tiny vessels, possibly used for medicines, to large containers capable of holding 20 to 30 litres. Most pots were decorated, usually with lines or other geometric motifs incised into the wet clay before the vessel was fired. Each Iroquoian village used its own distinctive style of decoration, and the relationships between villages can be traced by similarities in the types of decoration.

The Art of Captives

This kind of analysis can reveal some interesting information about the prehistoric Iroquoian peoples. For example, some of the pots recovered from late prehistoric Huron villages in central Ontario were decorated with distinctively St. Lawrence Iroquois designs, native to the upper St. Lawrence valley; conversely, pots with distinctively Huron designs were found occasionally on St. Lawrence Iroquois sites. In neither case, however, are there similarities in the styles of ceramic tobacco pipes that occur in each area. We know that in historic times cooking pots were made and decorated by Iroquoian women, whereas the men made and used the tobacco pipes that constituted the other major class of Iroquoian ceramics. The distribution of pottery among these villages suggests that there was considerably greater movement of women than of men between different villages, probably owing to the seventeenth-century Iroquoian warfare practice of adopting captured women and children into the victors' village (where the women continued to make pots as they had at home) and torturing and killing the men.

Iroquoian woman cooking over an open fire.

121

A second piece of evidence suggesting that the site was not Hochelaga is the predominance of beaver bones in the refuse collected by Dawson. On Iroquoian sites the most common mammal bones are those of deer; beaver became an important part of the local diet only after the establishment of trade relations with a European continent suddenly in love with felted beaver hats. Yet, considering Montréal Island's many low-lying areas and consequently large beaver population, how can we know that the local residents did not develop a taste for this very palatable rodent before the demand for beaver pelts?

Still a Mystery

Taking these facts into account, we must ultimately admit that archaeology can in no way prove the Dawson site to be the remains of Hochelaga. We know from Cartier's account that the town existed, and his vague description of its location fits the Dawson site as well as many other areas of Montréal Island. No other archaeological sites have been found on the island that could possibly represent the remains of Hochelaga. The Dawson site is either Hochelaga or the remains of a settlement very close in culture and time to that visited by Cartier. This is the only definite conclusion that archaeology can reach. Probably the most profitable approach is that assumed by Trigger in describing his fieldwork, which consisted of checking construction trenches, hiking over central Montréal to compare present landforms with those shown on old maps and studying the views from various parts of Mount Royal. "Perhaps the greatest pleasure gained from this study," he writes, "has been the opportunity to come to know my favourite city better."

CHAPTER 12

BUILDERS
OF
PLANK HOUSES

The archaeological remains of Canada's most impressive Indian villages, savaged by the destructive forces of the West Coast rain forest, are meagre reminders of the cultures that built them. The reconstruction of these prehistoric cultures involves a complex type of archaeology unique in Canada – the excavation of shell middens.

Carved stone bowl from the Queen Charlotte Islands.

The Pacific coast of British Columbia shows many faces. From the sea it can appear as a uniform wall of deep-green forest either clinging to bluff headlands or advancing to the tide line from a background of river valleys and rolling hills. To the visitor approaching it from inland, the coast is a pulsating scar of torn rock or flattened sand separating the calm of the forest from that of the sea beyond. As on most shorelines today, there are numerous signs of human activity: flotsam from fishing boats and offshore freighters, rusted logging machinery, and even concrete gun emplacements from the Second World War. The remains of abandoned settlements, logging camps, mines and canneries occupy many sheltered coves, but are rapidly disappearing under the encroaching forest as roofs collapse and trees take root on paths and in the buildings themselves.

In some of these settlements, the weathered stumps of carved poles and the fallen remains of rectangular wooden houses as big as logging-camp cookhouses or small canneries mark them as the locations of Indian villages abandoned during the past century. Like the gun emplacements and the worked-out mines, the villages are historical records of a way of life now vanished.

A Common Tradition

From northern California to southern Alaska, the temperate rain forests of the Pacific Coast are home to a variety of peoples known as the Northwest Coast Indians. That they speak languages belonging to several unrelated linguistic families bears testimony to a lengthy and complex history of settlement and occupation of the region. Yet, despite the diverse histories of these groups, their traditional ways of life resemble each other in many ways. There is evidence of extensive adaptation to similar environments and of the sharing of knowledge and techniques between groups all along the coast.

Carved house-posts in a Coast Salish house. The siding on this twentieth-century house is constructed of sawn boards.

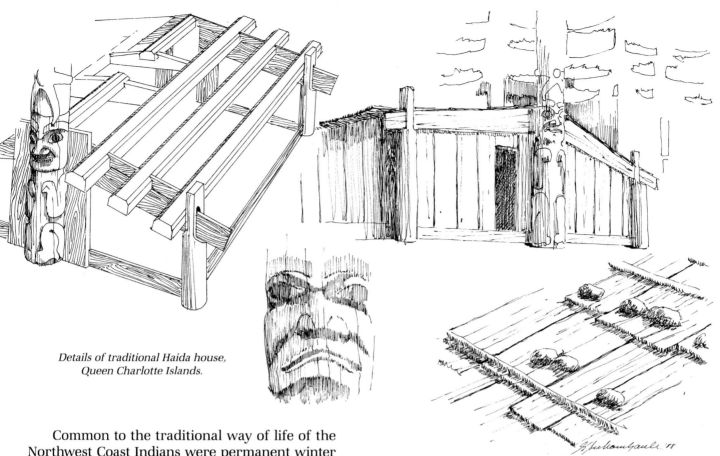

Details of traditional Haida house, Queen Charlotte Islands.

Common to the traditional way of life of the Northwest Coast Indians were permanent winter villages containing a number of large plank-walled houses, each occupied by extended families of 20 or more people. Some of these winter villages were home to several hundred, and their occupation was made possible by the storage of food supplies gathered in other seasons – when herring spawned, when salmon and eulachon ran in the local rivers or when offshore waters were calm enough for canoe visits to halibut banks or sea-lion rookeries. Indian groups spent much of these seasons in outcamps, living in temporary dwellings and transporting their surplus catches to their winter quarters. Despite this seasonal movement, the winter villages were occupied year-round by at least a few people, usually the elderly or disabled, who could best contribute to community life by acting as summer watchmen and perhaps minding the children who would have been in the way during the hectic work at summer fish-camps.

Diverse Architectural Styles

Although all winter houses of the Northwest Coast Indians were walled and roofed with large wooden planks supported by a framework of logs, their form varied considerably depending on local wood resources and traditions of construction. In the Strait of Georgia near present-day Van-

couver, the Coast Salish people built houses 6 to 8 metres wide and about 20 metres long. Each house had a low-pitched shed roof supported by massive upright posts. Walls were constructed of planks a metre or more wide, split from red cedar. The roof was made of similar planks, which could be shifted on fine days to provide light and allow smoke to escape. A plank platform ringed the interior walls and was divided into areas where individual families worked and slept. Cooking fires were built on the earth floor in the centre of the house, and the roof area held drying frames and food storage racks accessible by notched-log ladders.

On the stormy western coast of Vancouver Island, the Nootka built gable-roofed houses about 6 metres wide and 15 to 30 metres long, with the wall and roof planks overlapping and attached loosely to the frame so they could be easily removed. Many groups owned two or even three house frames located in areas where their annual round of hunting and fishing activities took them, and house planks were transported from one to another on the gunwales of two canoes, forming a type of catamaran to freight dried fish and other stores.

The most impressive villages of the region, however, were those built on the northern coast of British Columbia by the Haida of the Queen Charlotte Islands and the Tsimshian of the adjacent mainland coast. Tsimshian houses were 15 to 20 metres long on each side, with roof plates and floor sills mortised into huge upright cedar logs, vertical wall planks fitted into grooves in the plates and sills, and gable roofs supported by a pair of ridgepoles. Support posts were often carved into massive statuary, and the house front, facing the beach, was elaborately painted with family crests. Across Hecate Strait, Haida houses frequently had a huge house-pole built against the front wall, the mouth of the lowest figure on the carved pole serving as the door to the house. Haida villages, with their towering house-frontal, memorial and mortuary poles, and long rows of houses facing a beach lined with huge ocean-going canoes, were perhaps the most impressive settlements of aboriginal Canada. This was recently recognized when Anthony Island was declared a World Heritage Site. The small island is the site of Ninstints, a village occupied until the late nineteenth century and still containing some of the best-preserved examples of traditional Haida architecture and monumental art.

The House as Ancestor

To their occupants, villages such as these were not only home, but also metaphors for the structure of the world and man's place in it. The world was seen as a large plank house supported at the corners by huge poles; the night sky was a roof through whose holes sunlight shone as stars. On another level, the house was seen as the body of an ancestor: the spine was represented by the ridgepole, from which descended the rafters, representing ribs; these were supported by the limbs, represented by the house posts; and the face was a painting on the house front or the carved gable-end of the ridgepole. The arrangement of houses in the village reflected the social order of the community, with the house of the head chief at the centre and the houses of inferior ranks on the periphery. According to legend, the various kinds of animals lived in similar ranked villages, either in the forest or beneath the sea.

Over the past centuries, villages such as this marked many of the coves and inlets between Cape Mendocino and Yakutat Bay. Today the remains of many such villages lie beneath railway roadbeds, canning plants, harbour developments

Spindle whorls were used to spin the wool of mountain goats and dogs. This specimen, carved from black stone, is from a prehistoric Coast Salish site near Vancouver.

and the houses of modern towns and cities. Most of those escaping destruction at the hands of developers have been destroyed by the encroaching rain forest: seedlings sprout in the mouths of ancestral figures, their roots gradually tearing apart the entire sculpture; windfalls crush the frames of standing houses; and the continuous dampness beneath the forest canopy provides ideal conditions for the fungus growths that quickly reduce wood to humus. Since the Indian villages were built entirely of wood, it is not surprising that after a century or more of abandonment there is little on the surface of the forest floor to mark the site of these once-thriving communities.

The archaeologist studying prehistoric Northwest Coast Indians must accept the fact that the major part of their technology, including the tools, weapons and implements made of wood and other vegetable materials, will rarely be seen. With access to plentiful supplies of easily worked softwoods, the prehistoric craftsmen of the Northwest Coast created not only massive wooden houses, canoes and sculptures, but also containers and other items that in most parts of the world would have been made of other materials.

Basketry and matting of cedar bark and other materials made up another important but perishable group of artifacts fashioned by the Northwest Coast Indians. Only on a very few sites has this material been accidentally preserved by being waterlogged. Even the bones of animals used as food soon disappeared in the moist acidic soil of the forest floor. Most abandoned villages would be totally lost to us had not their inhabitants discarded large quantities of shellfish remains on the surfaces of the settlements.

A Dependable Food Supply

Although all Northwest Coast Indian groups gained most of their livelihood by fishing and by hunting sea and forest mammals, they also gathered shellfish, which in most areas were a dependable food resource throughout the year. Mussels, clams, cockles, limpets, sea urchins and other shellfish were collected, primarily by the women of the village, and during the lean winter months could provide an important or even a crucial part of the diet. Most shellfish were cooked by steaming in pits and could be smoked or dried and then stored in large wooden boxes for later use. The shells discarded in the vicinity of the houses became the major component of village refuse and served as a well-drained surface on which to live and to build later houses.

It is difficult to judge the importance of shellfish in the diet of the Northwest Coast Indians, especially those living in prehistoric times. In most villages it was probably of relatively minor importance except to add variety to the menu or provide sustenance in times of famine. A recent study of a group of Australian aborigines who have gone "back to the land" and are living on a diet similar to that of the traditional Northwest Coast Indians shows that, although shellfish collecting is a prominent activity, the shellfish provide only a very small proportion of their nutritional needs. Nevertheless, the large amount of shell discarded for each mouthful of meat consumed results in a very rapid accumulation of refuse. The archaeologist who does not take this into account could interpret the remains found in former coastal villages as an indication that the inhabitants lived almost entirely on shellfish.

Shell heaps were first recognized as evidence of ancient human habitation in nineteenth-century Denmark, when archaeologists began to excavate the remains of coastal Stone Age habitations. These features were called kitchen middens, the name applied to the heaps of refuse outside the doors of farmhouses; the term midden now applies to any ancient refuse pile. On the

continued page 132

Nineteenth-century Haida village in the Queen Charlotte Islands, with seagoing dugout canoes pulled up on the beach.

Totem Poles

The totem pole is a widely accepted symbol of native Canadian culture. It has gained this status only within the past century, probably beginning when the massive wood carvings of the British Columbia Indians were featured in the early promotional literature of the Canadian Pacific Railway. Many poles were bought from local families or stolen from abandoned villages and shipped to other parts of the country to stand in museums and public parks.

The large wood carvings known to the Canadian public as "totem poles" comprise a wide variety of objects, that had different uses and different meanings in the cultures that produced them. Some were house posts, integral parts of the massive plank houses of the Northwest Coast Indians. Others were mortuary poles, supporting large wooden boxes that contained the mortal remains of noble individuals. Still others were memorial poles raised in honour of particular people or events. All were carved with a series of heraldic crests, based on a complex system of patterns belonging to individual families or lineages. Similar crests were carved or painted on housefronts, canoes, masks, feast dishes and the large bentwood storage boxes of individual households. The practice of producing magnificent carvings in the traditional style continues today in British Columbia, where households, communities and museums commission them from native artists.

Such works of art stand in contrast to the vast numbers of "totem poles" carved by people with little knowledge or appreciation of the artistic traditions of the western rain forests. Often painted in garish colours unknown to aboriginal artists, such poles mark private businesses, shopping malls, Boy Scout headquarters and Indian band offices. Miniature versions whittled in wood or moulded in plastic, often imported from the Orient, are a staple of tourist gift shops, where they stand beside red-coated Mounties and maple sugar as symbols of Canada. They are deplorable travesties of a fine but poorly understood art form.

Details of totem poles.

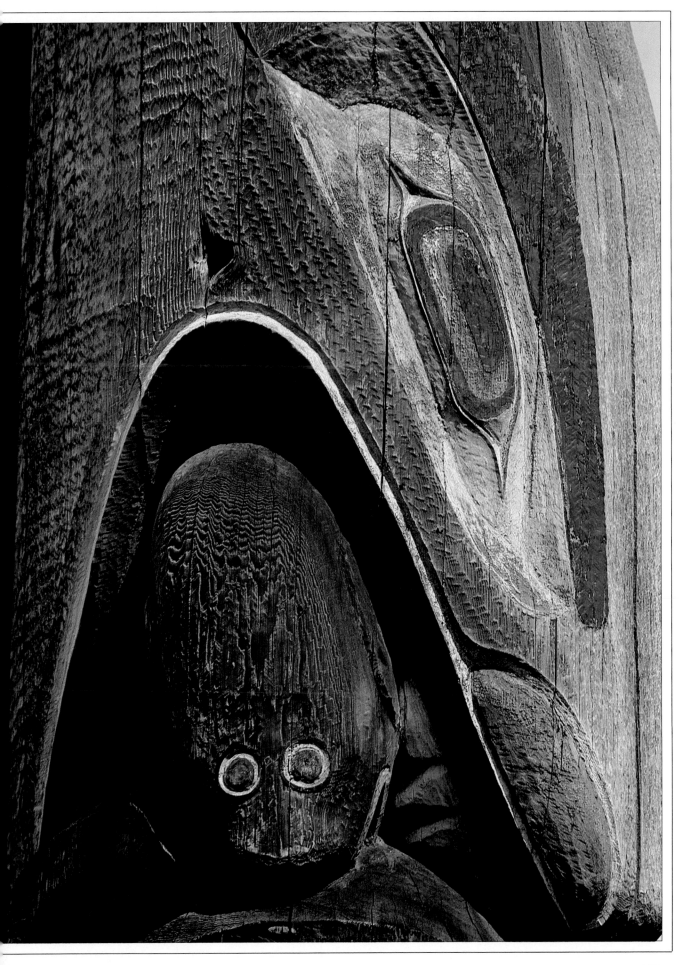

northwest coast, shell middens overgrown by dense forest are scattered along many coves and inlets. Some are small, representing the remains left by a few families living at a locality for only a few years. Others are truly immense: mounds several metres high containing thousands of cubic metres of shells and other refuse accumulated during an occupation period of up to 5 000 years. At least in their upper levels, these middens represent the remains of the large plank-walled houses described earlier. Some such sites are known to local inhabitants as the locations of villages occupied as recently as the present century.

excavation of house pits and storage or burial pits, and the sporadic moves of living areas from one portion of the midden surface to another – makes interpretation of the prehistoric record extremely difficult.

In excavating a shell midden, an archaeologist is faced with a bewildering array of features: deposits of shell ranging in size from a basketful, perhaps dumped by a child taking out the gar-

Ground-stone club.

Others have long been abandoned and come to the attention of archaeologists through coastal erosion, logging activities, road building and other construction. In the Prince Rupert Harbour area, planned expansion of port facilities during the 1970s led to a major salvage effort (carried out by George F. MacDonald, now director of the Canadian Museum of Civilization), in which over 200 sites were discovered and tested.

A Wealth of Information

The archaeological excavation of a major shell midden is a large-scale, time-consuming and often difficult exercise. The formation of these sites reveals a wealth of archaeological information. The calcium carbonate in the shells neutralizes the acidic groundwater characteristic of forest areas, thus preserving the bones of humans and animals (as well as artifacts made from bone and antler) buried in the midden. House floors, hearths and cooking pits are buried beneath later shell dumps, where they are protected from surface erosion. Portions of wooden house-posts and planks are occasionally recovered, but only in the upper levels of sites occupied during the last one or two hundred years; in the older levels of these sites the below-surface portions of house posts can often be traced as moulds of dark organic matter in the white shell matrix. However, the sheer complexity of past activity at such a site – the levelling of surfaces for house construction, the

bage after a family meal, to large beds, possibly the fill from the excavation of a house pit in a nearby area of the midden; flat strata of black organic matter that might be part of the floor of a house abandoned, then buried in shell, or merely what is left of a large woven mat discarded and thrown on the midden to rot; and pits that may have been excavated as footings for house posts, or simply as food caches. Since middens accumulated very gradually, the deposits close to the surface were often disturbed by later activities. Each level thus offers a very patchy picture of the midden surface at any one time in the past, with only discontinuous portions of each surface preserved for the archaeologist to see.

Development of a Complex Society

The difficulty in interpreting shell middens has led to considerable differences of opinion on the development of the Northwest Coast Indian way of life. Shell middens began to accumulate in most areas of the coast about 5 000 years ago, and marked the initial occupation of permanent or semipermanent villages. The establishment of these villages has been linked to the stabilization of river gradients at that time and the resulting establishment of large-scale salmon runs in coastal rivers. The fish and animal bones found in the lower levels of the middens indicate that these early people were already making use of most of the food resources in the region. However, there

continued on page 134

The Age of Wood

Stone Age, Bronze Age and Iron Age are convenient categories used by archaeologists to divide the past. They are based on the types of materials that have survived in the ground from ancient times until the present day. Yet, these terms should not obscure the fact that all of our ancestors for the past hundred thousand years or more lived in the "wood age". The most important uses of stone, bronze and iron were to chop trees, strip bark, cut or split planks, and fashion the wooden structures, vehicles and tools that until recently constituted the major portion of mankind's technology. Only in the latter half of the twentieth century (the plastic age, soon to be the ceramic age) have wood substitutes been produced on a large scale.

Like aboriginal populations around the world, the native peoples of Canada built and heated their houses with wood. All these peoples used wood and tree bark to construct their boats and had a detailed knowledge of the qualities that made each type of wood perfectly suited for carving a bow, a bowl or a cradle. Even the Inuit living on the treeless tundra went to great lengths to obtain wood through trade with the south, or driftwood logs that had come from the forests of Siberia.

Master Woodworkers

The master woodworkers of the New World lived on the Northwest Coast of North America, from northern California to southeastern Alaska. These diverse peoples all used the giant western cedar tree to fashion most of the their material goods. Standing up to 70 metres high and often 2 metres or more in diameter, the cedar has a soft shaggy bark, which can be used to make clothing, rope or mats, and a remarkably straight-grained soft wood, which can be split into planks several metres long.

Cedar trees first appeared in the coastal forests of western Canada about 5 000 years ago, shortly before the oldest known woodworking tools were developed. Before the invention of the chain saw, a standing cedar tree was a formidable adversary to men who wished to use its wood, and considerable ingenuity was applied to conquering it. One slow method of felling a tree was to set a fire at its base and chip away the charred timber as it burned. However, this was a tedious job, and for some purposes the tree did not have to be felled. Bark could be stripped in great sheets from a standing tree, and long planks could be split off by cutting notches at the upper and lower ends and then driving wedges into the wood. The coastal rain forests still contain living trees from which bark was stripped or planks split off over a century ago. Many living trees also contain the deep test holes that were cut to check if a tree had a rotten core before felling it for use as a canoe or a totem pole.

By the time of European contact, all Northwest Coast peoples possessed a complex woodworking technology: they worked with knife, adze and chisel blades of polished jade or other hard stone, wedges of wood or antler driven by carved stone mauls, drills with bone or stone points, and small tools made from the hard and sharp incisor teeth of beavers and porcupines. With such tools, the woodworkers of the Northwest Coast built their large plank houses and totem poles, and fashioned sea-going canoes up to 20 metres long from a single log. Masks, feast dishes and bent-wood boxes were carved in intricate patterns, which have been compared in complexity to those of ancient Greece. Such comparisons are too subjective to qualify as valid artistic criticism. However, we can be fairly certain that the native people of British Columbia, after 5 000 years of honing their skills on cedar trees, are among the greatest woodworkers the world has yet produced.

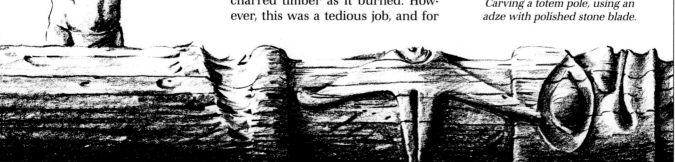

Carving a totem pole, using an adze with polished stone blade.

is no evidence at these levels of large plank-walled houses, nor of the totemic art that in the Historic period was intimately tied to the complex system of wealth and social ranking at the basis of traditional Northwest Coast Indian society.

About 3 000 years ago, middens were accumulating more rapidly in some areas, suggesting increased populations; in addition, finds of occasional art objects and exotic trade goods are taken by some archaeologists to indicate the development of the complex social organization characteristic of the Historic period. Others consider that this development occurred more gradually, and that the complex economy and society of the Northwest Coast Indians evolved only during the millennium before European contact. The large multifamily houses with carved house posts or painted house fronts were an integral part of the social organization of the Northwest Coast Indians. Given the complexity of midden excavation, however, it is to be expected that the remains of large plank-walled houses, such as those occupied during the Historic period, are very difficult to trace in the prehistoric past.

As most archaeological work on the Northwest Coast Indian sites has taken place during the past two decades, it is perhaps not surprising that we still know relatively little about a way of life probably richer and more sophisticated than any developed by other non-agricultural peoples of the world. Most archaeological work is now devoted to salvaging the remnants of prehistory on sites threatened by development. Let us hope that the coming decades will bring not only more information on the prehistory of the Northwest Coast Indians, but also a concerted attempt to preserve this portion of the Canadian heritage.

CHAPTER 13

FARMERS OF THE GREAT LAKES

The aboriginal farming nations of Ontario are known to us only through the accounts of a few seventeenth-century explorers and missionaries. To add to this knowledge, we must turn to archaeology.

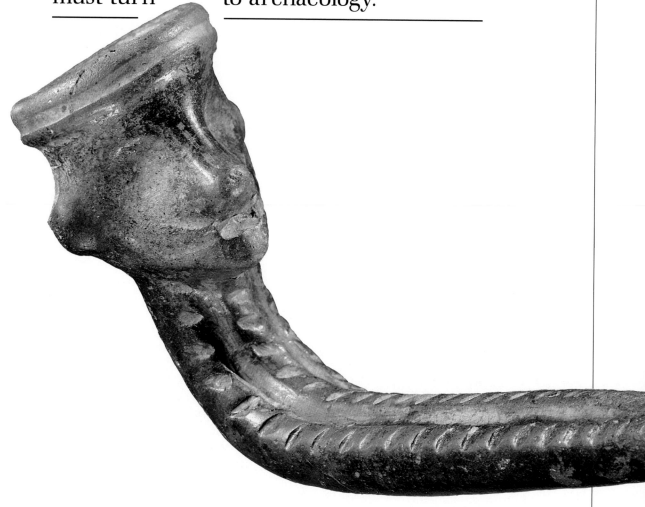

Pottery smoking-pipe, from a late-prehistoric Iroquoian site.

On a hot spring afternoon a plough slices through grass and wild flowers in a field. Only a few acres in extent, this awkward triangle of ground between two converging ravines was abandoned by the farmer's grandfather when he bought his first tractor and found it less manoeuvrable than a team of horses. In the light loam soil being turned by the plough, the farmer notices a few patches of red or grey soil, perhaps the remains of burned stumps. In one such patch, however, his eye is caught by a scatter of small objects. Stopping the tractor and stooping to the furrow, he finds bits of charred animal bone, a few sharp-edged chips of flinty stone, and some flat reddish-brown objects resembling pieces of a broken flowerpot. Turning one of them over, he notices that its surface is decorated with a deeply impressed hatching of diagonal lines. He has seen such decorated sherds before, in a basket at the back of the old woodshed, and remembers his grandfather's stories of an old Indian village somewhere at the back of the farm. Another archaeological site has been discovered.

Villages of More than 2 000 People

When the farmer's ancestors first homesteaded this land in the early nineteenth century, all of southern Ontario was heavily forested, and inhabited by a few small groups of Indians who hunted, fished, and trapped for the fur trade. These people spoke Algonquian languages, and their traditional home was in the coniferous forests to the north.

When Samuel de Champlain first penetrated the region in 1615, he described quite a different country and population. Having travelled through the forested Algonquian country along the Ottawa and French river systems, he entered the homeland of his Huron hosts. This region, which became known as Huronia, stretched approximately 50 kilometres from east to west and 30 kilometres from north to south, between Lake Simcoe and Georgian Bay. About 20 000 people lived in this small area, and signs of human activity were everywhere. Large areas of forest had been cleared, leaving extensive grasslands, and every few kilometres there was a village surrounded by the fields of maize, beans and squash that provided the 1 000 to 2 000 inhabitants with most of their subsistence.

The people spoke a language of the Iroquoian family, and both their language and customs were related to those of the agricultural peoples living south of the Great Lakes. They were not the only Iroquoian group in Ontario. A few kilometres to the west, along the southwestern shores of Georgian Bay, lived their allies the Petun, or Tobacco Nation. To the south, around the western end of Lake Ontario, were the people known to the French as the Neutrals, since they remained aloof from the wars between the Hurons and the Iroquois of what is now New York State. To the east, Iroquoian farmers had inhabited the upper St. Lawrence valley at the time of Jacques Cartier's visit in 1534, but had disappeared by Champlain's time, probably as a result of warfare related to the early fur trade. The Hurons had also been influenced by the fur trade. They called themselves Wendat, meaning the people who live on a peninsula, and the name referred to a confederacy of four tribes, or nations, that had joined together in Huronia during the sixteenth century. Prior to that time, some of the ancestral Huron had lived in the Trent River valley and along the shores of Lake Ontario. They probably moved north to obtain easier access to the furs trapped by their northerly Algonquian neighbours and to the Ottawa River trade route to the French in the St. Lawrence valley.

Witnesses of the Past

All of these Iroquoian peoples led essentially similar ways of life, but more is known of the Hurons from descriptions by Champlain and the Jesuit missionaries who lived among them until their destruction or dispersal in the late 1640s by the Iroquois of what is now New York State. Over the past several decades, archaeological work in Huron country has added to our knowledge and clarified many of the early descriptions. Champlain counted 18 inhabited villages during the winter he spent in Huronia, some of which can be identified archaeologically. Other archaeological sites represent villages not mentioned by the early chroniclers. While Huron communities were of considerable duration, the villages occupied by these communities lasted only one or two decades before being abandoned. The Hurons abandoned a village when the fertility of the local soil decreased, or when the local forests were so depleted that firewood could no longer be collected nearby. New villages were generally built several kilometres from the old, the forests were cleared by burning and new fields prepared for crops, which would flourish for a few years until

136

continued page 142

The Culinary Art

A shared taste for certain foods is a major element defining human societies. Our tastes are developed in childhood and continue to influence our choice of foods – whether it be raw fish, or macaroni and cheese – throughout life. Although most people like to try the foods of other cultures, and enjoy them as a treat on occasion, their everyday diet generally remains conservative. When people are transplanted into another society, one marked symptom of "culture shock" is an aversion to the new diet.

The seventeenth-century Jesuit missionaries, transported from French seminaries to the villages of the Hurons, had little to say in favour of the food provided by their hosts. It is now evident from their journals and reports that these early missionaries suffered from varying degrees of culture shock. Their complaints are remarkably similar to those of modern northern natives who, as children, had to reside for months on end in mission schools, where they were fed such alien foods as milk, oatmeal, cabbage and carrots. When reading early European accounts of native cuisine we must make allowance for the authors' cultural biases, which are perhaps more conspicuous than in their descriptions of other aspects of native life.

A Varied Cuisine

The cuisine of aboriginal America was much more diverse than we might expect. An estimated 2 000 species of native American plants and animals were used as food. Included were many domestic plants that have since become part of the European diet: corn, beans, tomatoes, squash, pumpkins, sunflowers and potatoes.

In the Mexico of the Aztecs, the common people subsisted on much the same sort of food served today in Mexican restaurants, while the nobility enjoyed elaborate confections based on chocolate, chili peppers, pineapples, domestic fowls, and numerous wild plants, animals and fish. The Kwakiutl people of coastal British Columbia had over 150 recipes for preparing local fish, shellfish, birds, mammals and plants. The Inuit of Arctic Canada, whose environment provided only a few species of animals or edible plants and little firewood for cooking or otherwise processing food, managed to enjoy a surprisingly varied diet. A single food item – Arctic char, for example – could be eaten fresh (either raw or boiled), frozen, dried, packed in seal oil, or stored in cool rock caches until it acquired the taste and consistency of old cheese. Although lichens are not edible in their raw form, they were tasty and nutritious in a processed form as found in the stomach of a freshly-killed caribou.

Throughout most of aboriginal Canada, people lived almost entirely on meat. A wide variety of vegetable foods – nuts, seeds, berries, roots, seaweeds, salad greens, the inner bark of trees – was known, but was used primarily to add variety to the diet. Only during times of starvation – in summers when an expected run of fish did not appear or in winters when no animals could be found – did plants assume an important role. A few groups depended more heavily on plant foods: in the interior of British Columbia the tuberous roots of the camas plant were important, as was wild rice in parts of the eastern woodlands.

Agricultural Subsistence

Living on the extreme northern limit of aboriginal North American agriculture, the Iroquoians of southern Ontario and the St. Lawrence valley were the only native peoples in Canada who depended on cultivated plants for most of their livelihood. Their crops consisted of plants that are native to the subtropics – primarily corn, beans and squashes that had been domesticated in Mexico or Central America as early as 7 500 years ago. These plants could not be cultivated in Canada until farmers had developed varieties that would mature in the relatively short frost-free season of a Canadian summer. The cultivation of corn first appeared in southern Ontario sometime between A.D. 500 and 1000; beans and squash were added about A.D. 1400. By the time of European exploration, these three crops provided approximately 80 per

A potter finishes the rim of a pot she will use to cook meals in for her family. Iroquoian pottery was modelled by hand rather than turned on a wheel.

cent of the diet of the Hurons and probably of other northern Iroquoian peoples as well.

The Hurons ate twice a day, in the morning and evening. The main daily dish was a soup made from cornmeal, which also contained beans, squash, fish or meat, according to the recipe followed and the ingredients available. Women ground the corn in large wooden mortars with a heavy hardwood pestle. The soup was then cooked in pottery vessels set on an open fire. At least occasionally a neglected pot of soup boiled dry and burned, and the cooking pot had to be thrown away. Archaeologists have been able to reconstruct the menu of the day from such pots, encrusted with a thick layer of carbonized cornmeal, beans, and fish bones. Cornmeal was also used in unleavened bread, with dried berries or deer fat added to the dough. When travelling or on war parties, Huron men carried only a pouch of cornmeal, which they ate dry; the French were amazed at the speed that a party could achieve and the distance it could cover on such a small and portable quantity of food. They were less impressed with a Huron party dish prepared by soaking small, immature ears of corn in a pond until they fermented.

A More Advanced Society?

We tend to think of agricultural peoples as more progressive than those who live by hunting and fishing. However, the progress made by the Hurons in adopting farming as a mode of life was accompanied by several drawbacks. On the positive side, the Hurons were probably more secure from famine than were their neighbours who depended on hunting and fishing. Although the crops did occasionally fail, large amounts of corn appear to have been stored as protection against such a calamity, and for trade with neighbouring groups in return for fish and furs. Agriculture allowed the Hurons to live in more densely populated communities than could other aboriginal Canadian peoples. However, to support the estimated 20 000 Hurons who occupied the small area between Lake Simcoe and Georgian Bay, approximately 7 000 acres of crops had to be planted, tended, weeded and harvested. Recent anthropological studies of agricultural peoples living much like the Hurons indicate that these tasks require far more time and effort than does hunting. In fact, hunting groups have been termed "the original affluent societies", their affluence consisting of leisure time and its related pleasures. On the other hand, they face a certain degree of insecurity about where the next day's meals will come from.

Among the Hurons and other non-industrial farming peoples, agriculture did not produce a more enjoyable or more nutritious diet than that of their hunting ancestors. The state of the teeth in skeletons recovered from prehistoric sites shows that agriculture was a mixed blessing. While the teeth of most prehistoric peoples would be the envy of modern Canadians, the teeth of almost all Hurons were riddled with caries and abscesses. If toothache was an almost constant fact of life among the Hurons – which it probably was – it can be traced directly to their diet.

A Monotonous Diet

As for taste and enjoyment, we may imagine that corn soup, regardless of the care and effort involved in its preparation, provided a much more monotonous diet than that available in most hunting camps. Hunters may have eaten a breakfast of smoked fish, a few snacks of berries or cold meat, and a supper of roast goose or boiled venison stew. This is the kind of food so sorely missed by native children placed in boarding schools. The Hurons who first adopted agriculture must also have longed for such food. Corn provided security against famine and allowed people to live in much larger and denser communities. But, as elsewhere around the world, agriculture made people work harder, made their teeth ache and probably added little to the daily enjoyment of life.

Interior of a Huron longhouse. Heat and light were provided by a number of central fires, each tended and used by the families who occupied adjacent living areas along either wall. Corn, the staple of the Huron diet, was stored on lines hung from the ceiling of the house.

the soil was drained of nutrients. The cycle of village abandonment and rebuilding would then begin again.

Such a living pattern results in a large number of village sites, each representing a small slice of the history of a particular Huron community. Today there is little or nothing to be seen on the surface of these sites. Most of them lie in flat agricultural fields, close to water and often on high ground between two converging ravines – a location easily defended with a log palisade. Scattered across such a site, mainly along the edges of the ravines, are the remains of middens, where ashes, animal bones, broken pots and other refuse were dumped. The palisades and houses of the village, if not destroyed or carried off to be used in the construction of a new village, cannot have lasted more than a few decades after the village was abandoned. Their outlines can, however, be traced in the light-coloured subsoil below the levels disturbed by farmers' ploughs. They are identified by series of small circular patches of darker soil, which are post moulds marking where vertical posts had been driven deeply into the soil and either rotted in place or were removed, allowing darker topsoil to collapse into the hole.

By scraping away the topsoil and plotting post moulds, hearth pits, storage pits and other features, archaeologists can obtain a detailed plan of the entire village. This plan shows the village was surrounded by several lines of stakes representing a defensive palisade, which enclosed a number of elongated rectangles with rounded ends (often arranged in one or more parallel rows). These are the remains of longhouse dwellings, usually about 8 metres wide and 20 to 30 metres long, although some houses more than twice that length have been found.

The Huron Longhouse

A combination of archaeological evidence and historical description makes it possible to reconstruct the Huron longhouse. The outer wall was formed of long upright poles driven into the ground and covered with sheets of bark; the roof, approximately ten metres high, was either gabled or arched, with holes to allow the smoke of cooking fires to escape. A series of hearths extended down the middle of the house, each fire used by the two families in its vicinity, who occupied opposite wall areas. The side walls were lined with

Plan of an Iroquoian longhouse, uncovered at the village of Lanoraie near Montréal. The black dots outlining the earthen floor represent post moulds left by upright poles that formed the walls. The coloured patches in the interior show the locations of hearths and of pits used for burying debris and perhaps for storage.

platforms for sleeping and working, each family having its own section. Food and firewood were stored in the rounded end-sections of the house, and corn and dried fish were hung on cords from the roof. The ends of the houses were painted, probably with family crests. In each village, at least one longhouse was larger than the rest and was used for councils, games and other communal activities. These houses generally belonged to chiefs, who had obtained positions of prestige, either through inheritance or through their accomplishments as leaders in hunting or warfare.

Houses were occupied by about five to ten families, usually related through the female line; this longhouse community was the basic social and economic unit of Huron society. The mother and daughters or the group of sisters whose families lived together cooperated in gathering firewood and growing the crops, so that each longhouse was more or less self-sufficient in food and fuel. Men had broader allegiances, but those who shared a longhouse worked together in its construction and probably tended to cooperate in fishing and hunting to supply the group of families with meat. In summer the men were often away on extended hunting, trading or war expeditions, while the women spent much of their time in the fields. In the winter, however, the village was the centre of all activity, as there was little work to be done and usually enough stored food to last until spring.

The Jesuit missionaries' accounts paint a picture of such villages huddled in a snowy landscape, the houses filled with wood smoke, noise, unwashed bodies and dogs. When the crops were destroyed by poor weather or, more commonly, by Iroquois raiding parties from south of Lake Ontario, hunger overshadowed the picture. Epidemic diseases afflicted the villages more frequently as contacts with the French increased. The French had little praise for what they considered an appallingly squalid way of life.

Unquestionably, some of the difficulties of Huron life resulted from involvement in the fur trade. Epidemic diseases had probably not been prevalent before the seventeenth century, nor had

continued page 146

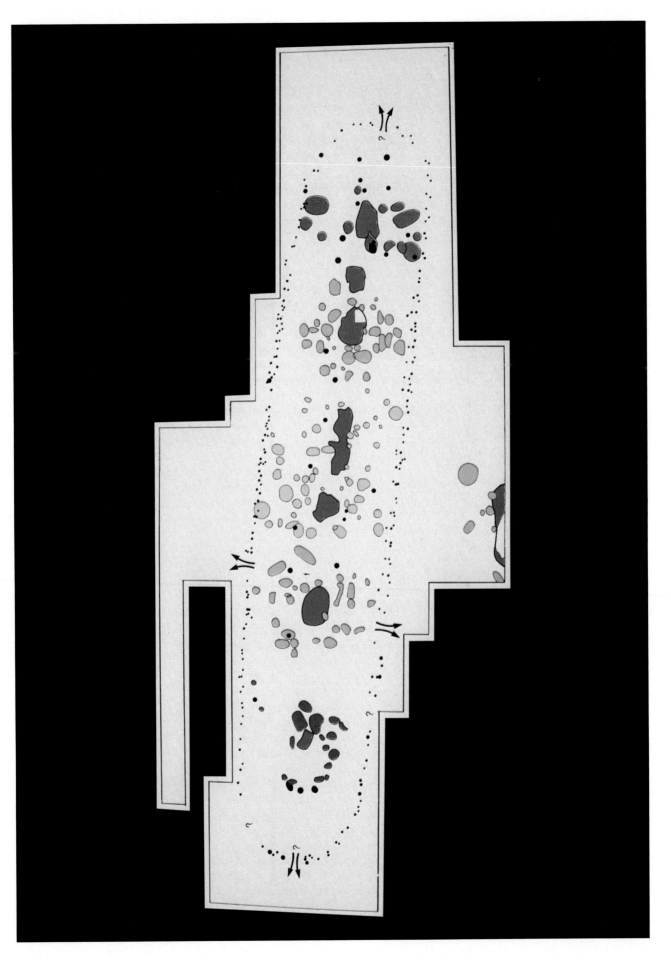

143

A Matriarchal Society

The terms "matriarchy" and "patriarchy" are very vaguely defined. Current feminist rhetoric holds that a patriarchal society is one in which men dominate all fields, and in which women are expected to be submissive. In matriarchal society, women should therefore be similarly dominant. However, there is no society on earth in which all decisions are made by one sex and submissively accepted by the other.

The early European explorers of North America came from a society that could be called "patriarchal". The more precise anthropological terms for European societies are "patrilineal" (in which inheritance of property, positions and titles follows the male line, as reflected in the European tradition of women taking the family name of their husbands) and "patrilocal" (meaning that, upon marrying, the woman generally moves to the home of her husband). This type of society is thought to have developed when ancient Indo-Europeans were herders of horses, sheep and cattle on the plains of western Asia. In such a society, where the animals were herded by men, it was natural for family wealth in the form of animals to pass from father to son. It was also convenient for women to join the families of their husbands, who were caring for flocks still owned by their fathers. Over the millennia, as Europeans became farmers and then urbanites, the economy changed, but the rules of inheritance and family residence remained the same, though they became less rigidly observed.

When Champlain and the French missionaries of the early seventeenth century encountered the Hurons, they found a society organized along quite different lines. Huron women owned most of the major goods – houses, crops and fields – in their community. The birth of a girl was more welcomed than that of a boy, since she would grow up to increase the size and strength of the matrilineal clan. When he married, a Huron man left his home and joined that of his wife. The Huron longhouse, which typically housed six families, was the basic social unit; ideally, it was occupied by a mother and her daughters, or by a group of sisters, along with their husbands and children. On a larger scale, the most important social unit was the clan, consisting of all those who traced their descent from a common female ancestor. All Hurons traced their ancestry to Aataentsic, the mother of mankind, a female spirit who had fallen from the sky.

Very Different Rules

Although one might expect the political leaders of such a society to be female, Huron politics were publicly conducted by a group of male chiefs. The matrilineal clan of each Huron village had a civil chief and a war chief, whose dealings with each other and the chiefs of other villages involved elaborate protocols. In theory, the office of chief was hereditary; it was passed not to a man's son, but to his sister's son so that it remained within the matrilineage. However, hereditary chieftainship could lead to problems when the heir was young, inexperienced or untrustworthy. If Huron tradition was like that of other Iroquoian peoples on whom we have more information, the women of the matrilineal clan had the authority to depose an unpopular chief and elect a new one. The public authority of Huron men was judiciously balanced by the more private authority of women.

Like the economic argument that the patrilineal and patrilocal rules of European society grew out of the conditions of ancient herding peoples, a similar argument might explain the matrilineal and matrilocal rules of Huron society: the Hurons derived approximately 80 per cent of their food from agriculture. Women were the farmers, spending most of the spring and summer planting, protecting and harvesting the fields of corn, beans and squash. The remaining 20 per cent of the society's food was provided by the fishing and hunting activities of the men. Another important consideration is that girls grew up helping their mothers to tend a certain set of fields. Farmers know their own land better than that of their neighbours, and are more efficient in dealing with its subtle characteristics over the long term than they would be if they moved to another farm. A Huron woman was attached to her fields by both knowledge and sentiment; marriage was not a sufficient reason to break this attachment, and the matrilocal residence rule allowed her to retain her own fields. As men moved to the homes of their wives, away from the support of their own families and into a social unit consisting of their wife's mother and sisters, women naturally wielded a great deal of social power.

A Subtle Balance of Power

The economic explanation for a society's choice of organization along

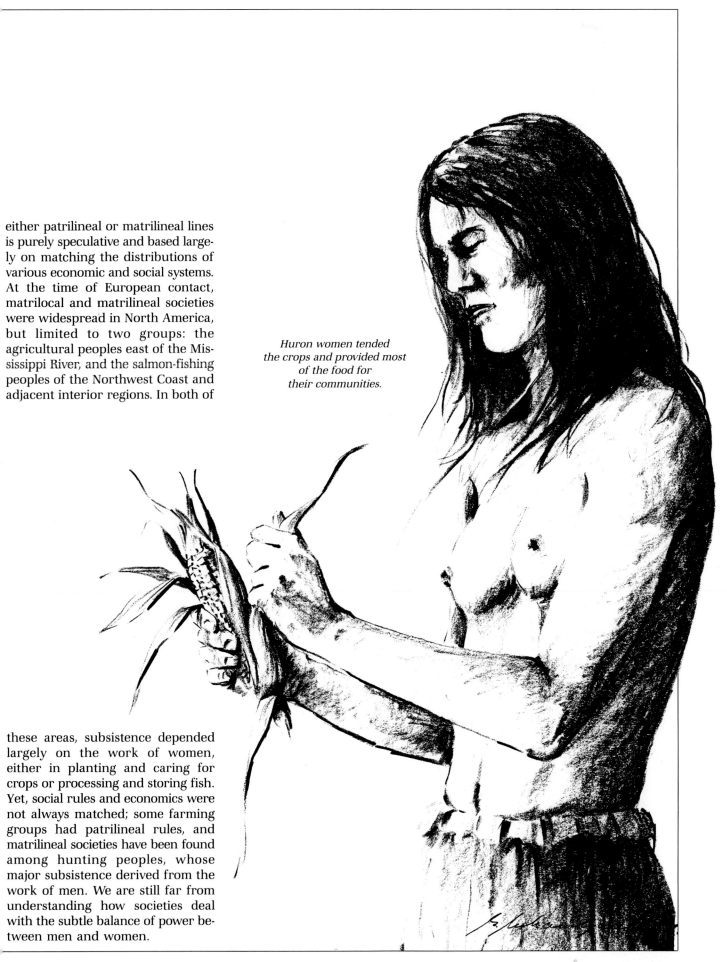

either patrilineal or matrilineal lines is purely speculative and based largely on matching the distributions of various economic and social systems. At the time of European contact, matrilocal and matrilineal societies were widespread in North America, but limited to two groups: the agricultural peoples east of the Mississippi River, and the salmon-fishing peoples of the Northwest Coast and adjacent interior regions. In both of

Huron women tended the crops and provided most of the food for their communities.

these areas, subsistence depended largely on the work of women, either in planting and caring for crops or processing and storing fish. Yet, social rules and economics were not always matched; some farming groups had patrilineal rules, and matrilineal societies have been found among hunting peoples, whose major subsistence derived from the work of men. We are still far from understanding how societies deal with the subtle balance of power between men and women.

aboriginal warfare been as continuous or as devastating as the wars that grew around the fur-trade routes to the eastern coast. Most other aspects of Huron life, however, were part of an old pattern developed in Ontario over the previous millennium. It was the northern fringe of a widespread pattern of Indian life that had advanced northwards from Meso-America with the spread of agriculture, finally reaching southern Ontario about A.D. 500. As knowledge of agriculture spread northwards out of Mexico and as cultivated plants became adapted to more-northerly climates, most Indian groups living in arable regions became farmers. But in more-northerly areas agriculture was less productive and therefore less capable of supporting dense populations, a prerequisite for the development of highly structured systems of social organization. The civilizations of Mexico, centralized states based on the intensive cultivation of a wide variety of crops, never spread northwards into the present United States. Yet evidence of elements of their way of life, including political organizations that were possibly rudimentary states, and towns with central plazas and large earthen temple mounds, have been found as far north as the Ohio Valley. In Ontario, where agriculture was even more difficult, politics were handled by clan and village organizations. The need for broader organization was met in the sixteenth century by confederacies such as those formed by the Huron and other Iroquoian groups to settle intertribal quarrels and provide defensive alliances in case of war. Among the Iroquois, the social organization of the multifamily longhouse was seen as a model for such widespread confederacies.

Communal Houses

The longhouse, or a variant of it, seems to be closely associated with the type of forest agriculture practised by the Hurons. Some South American Indian groups of the Amazon region still live in such large communal dwellings. In Europe, archaeological sites of the Neolithic period, of 5 000 years ago and earlier, show the same patterns of post moulds outlining large communal houses and palisaded villages that were occupied for a few years and then abandoned, probably for the same reasons as were those of the Hurons. There is no historical connection between these forms of houses and villages in the Old and New Worlds. However, there seems to be a common social factor: the communal dwelling, occupied by a group of related families, probably served to bond a so-cial and economic unit that could operate efficiently under the conditions of primitive forest agriculture. Regardless of the origin of our ancestors, archaeology shows that they almost certainly at some time lived in longhouses resembling those of the Hurons.

CHAPTER 14

THE DEFENCE OF KITWANGA

A hilltop on the upper Skeena River bears the remains of a fortified settlement. Built by a famed Gitksan chief and warrior, it is a reminder of the trading wars that followed the introduction of iron and other European materials to the Northwest Coast.

Stone club from a cache found on the upper Skeena River.

The northern interior of British Columbia is veined by a network of ancient pathways, the "grease trails" built and maintained over the centuries by the Indian inhabitants of the area. Many of the early European explorers of the region were escorted along these trails, across the rivers on suspension bridges and past numerous villages and occasional forts. Kitwanga is one such fort, located at the headwaters of the Skeena River a few kilometres west of Hazelton. In 1971 Kitwanga was declared a National Historic Site, and in 1979 archaeological excavations were carried out by George F. MacDonald on behalf of Parks Canada, the custodians of the site. The results of the archaeological dig, interpreted with the aid of local traditional knowledge of the occupation and use of the site, show that fortresses, and the complex political and economic circumstances that made them necessary, were a part of Indian as well as European life in early Canada.

An Ingenious Defence System

The Kitwanga fortress lies on the flat top of a small, steep hill rising 25 metres from the banks of the Kitwanga River. According to local tradition the hill is man-made, but excavations show that the builders constructed their fortified village on an unusual geological feature, where they could easily defend themselves. Around the rim of the hilltop they built a log palisade; according to legend, this was reinforced by an ingenious arrangement of large spiked logs that could be rolled down the hill onto attackers.

On top of the hill, the remains of five large houses have been found, those at each end supported by stilts so that they jutted out over the hillside. The houses appear to have been large, rectangular plank structures with gable roofs and central hearths, similar to houses of Historic-period Gitksan villages found in the same area. The Kitwanga houses, however, had some additional features: hidden beneath their floor planks were large pits, apparently for food storage. Along the back walls of the houses were shallower pits, designed as hiding places for women and children and equipped with trapdoors to allow escape through tunnels beneath the palisade if the fort were taken. MacDonald estimates that the area within the palisade contains the remains of over 1 000 pits in which dried salmon, meats and berries were stored in case of siege. Larger food-storage pits were discovered around the foot of the hill; according to tradition, these pits were constructed and filled with food by individual women, who camouflaged them and kept their locations secret so that an enemy could not force any one person to reveal the location of more than a few pits.

A Commercial Network

Kitwanga is only one of a hundred such forts, and certainly not the largest, that existed in northern British Columbia and southern Alaska in the period shortly before European exploration of the area. What social and economic conditions necessitated the building of such fortified structures? MacDonald suggests that the forts were an outgrowth of the trade networks that had been established throughout the area for at least 2 000 years and of the ownership systems that evolved over this period. The ownership of property by individuals, families or clans was highly developed and very important to all Northwest Coast Indians. The bridges, forts and trails of the trading network were owned by individual chiefs or families, who could levy tolls and exercise control over the traders using their property.

At first the trails were probably used primarily to transport foodstuffs and other basic commodities between the coast and the interior and between different regions of the interior. The most famous trail was the Kitwankul, which leads past the fort of Kitwanga. It was used mainly to transport eulachon grease from the Nass River to the villages of the Skeena. The eulachon is a small fish, from which was extracted an oil that was an important part of Indian diet in that area. According to tradition, the people who owned the eulachon fishery on the Nass River freely invited others to help themselves to a seemingly inexhaustible resource, and, similarly, free passage of eulachon grease was allowed on the Kitwankul trail. Nineteenth-century European travellers along this trail record meeting large numbers of Indians returning from the fishery, heavily laden with great wooden boxes of grease.

Free passage, however, was not extended to other and more precious goods. Exotic materials such as obsidian, native copper and abalone shell had probably formed a small part of aboriginal trade along this and other trails, but by the early eighteenth century new and more valuable goods were beginning to appear in the area. The first European traders reached the northwest coast in

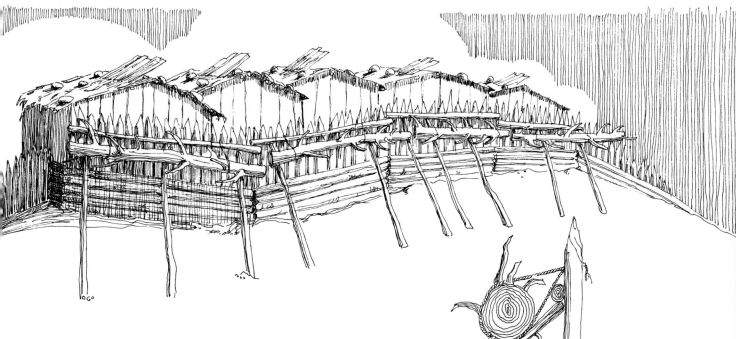

*Artist's reconstruction of Kitwanga Fort,
with detail of rolling-log
defences described in oral tradition.*

the 1770s, the English and Spanish coming from the south and the Russians from their recently established posts in Alaska. All these traders and explorers, including the first Russians to visit Alaska in the 1740s, reported that the use of iron was already established in the area. Although some metal goods may have originated in the Spanish colonies in Mexico and California or in English and French trading posts far to the east of the mountains, MacDonald thinks that most arrived through intertribal trade across the Bering Strait. Throughout the seventeenth century, Russian fur-traders and explorers pushed rapidly eastwards across Siberia, and by 1700 Russian trade goods had reached the coast of the Bering Sea. Here, Chukchi traders passed valuable iron and copper objects to their Alaskan Eskimo trading partners, who no doubt found them desirable items for trade in turn with their Indian neighbours to the south.

According to MacDonald, the appearance of these new commodities eventually transformed the aboriginal politics of northern British Columbia. Among the peoples of both the coast and the interior there seems to have been a general northward movement, perhaps to gain greater access to the new trade goods and the profits possible from retrading the goods to peoples with less access to them. Ownership of the trading trails and bridges now became increasingly lucrative, and forts such as Kitwanga began to appear throughout the area to protect this ownership, enforce tolls and control trade. From these secure havens, chiefs and families built up their wealth through trade and through warfare against the owners of other forts. Thus was laid the foundation of the great monopolistic trading chiefdoms of the nineteenth century.

A Warrior Architect

Only in very special cases can archaeologists name the person who built a prehistoric settlement, and Kitwanga is one such case. The legends of the Gitksan people, recorded by Marius Barbeau over 50 years ago and supplemented by the knowledge of present Gitksan residents of the area, tell a great deal about the *Ta'awdzep*, or hill fort, at Kitwanga. These legends describe a warrior named Nekt, from the Queen Charlotte Islands, the son of a Haida chief and a high-ranking Gitksan woman who had been captured during a Haida raid. Nekt's mother is said to have killed her husband and escaped to the mainland with her infant son, who grew into a wild and reckless boy and was finally expelled from the village by his

A dispute over access to trade routes leads to an attack on Kitwanga Fort. The attackers use arrows and fire, while the defenders rely on their stockade and its unique rolling-log defences.

Smokehouses and bridge built in traditional patterns on the upper Skeena River.

mother's brothers. After a period of wandering in the forest, Nekt fell in with a group of families who were the ancestors of the Kitwanga people. Having acquired a magical war club and a suit of impenetrable armour made from the skin of a grizzly bear and covered with pitch and flakes of slate, he began raiding coastal and river settlements, where he was mistaken for a mythical grizzly bear whose attacks could not be resisted.

Nekt is alleged to have built the hill fort of Kitwanga and equipped it with the log rollers and trapdoors he saw in a dream. His identity was eventually learned by the victims of his raids, who formed a confederacy to destroy him. He was finally killed by a bullet, from which his armour could not protect him, and his fort was destroyed. Some say that the bullet was fired from the first gun seen in the area.

Archaeology cannot confirm or deny the truth of the Nekt legend, but findings generally

bear out the details of the legend. For example, the 1979 dig recovered evidence of hiding places beneath the rear floor areas of the houses, perhaps connected to the trapdoor escape routes seen by Nekt in his dream. A comparison of the tree rings of wood and charcoal found at Kitwanga with those of living trees shows that the site was burned and abandoned in the 1830s – at about the time that the first Hudson's Bay Company posts were established in the area and efficient guns became readily available. This is consistent with the time when, according to legend, Nekt died. Although archaeological evidence indicates that the settlement had been in use for at least a century, it was at some time expanded from a single house to the five houses that were perhaps enclosed by Nekt's palisade. The expansion may have represented the growing power and increased need for security of a local warrior chief. It is reasonable to assume that there was a man named Nekt, who either built or expanded the hill fort at Kitwanga, and perhaps that his ambition and success as a raider led to the final destruction of the fort by his victims and enemies.

Bridges such as this once linked the grease trails throughout coastal British Columbia.

The period of the hill forts in northern British Columbia lasted little more than a century. By the end of this time firearms had made the forts obsolete, populations had begun to decline because of epidemic diseases, and a few coastal chiefs who quickly subdued their lesser rivals were beginning to consolidate power. Forts such as Kitwanga belong to a little-known period of Canadian history. It was a time when aboriginal ways of life were being rapidly changed, often destabilized and occasionally destroyed by the indirect influence of European expansion – an influence that spread hundreds or even thousands of kilometres ahead of the Europeans themselves.

CHAPTER 15

BELUGA HUNTERS

At the mouth of the Mackenzie River, on the coast of the Western Arctic, lie the remains of the largest Inuit village in Canada. During the past few centuries, up to a thousand people lived here each summer hunting beluga whales, catching them in a unique natural trap.

Ivory harpoon head excavated from the midden at Kittigazuit.

Most of the world's major rivers have a great city located at their outlet to the sea: Alexandria on the Nile, New Orleans on the Mississippi, and Shanghai on the Yangtze. People were probably first drawn to river mouths, several thousands of years ago, by the excellent fishing generated by the mingling of warm and nutrient-rich fresh water with the cooler water of the sea. With the development of agriculture, the fine rich soils of river deltas made such locations prime farming country. Before the existence of road systems, rivers were the main transportation routes into the interiors of most continents, and with the establishment of large-scale maritime trade, river mouths became the points where goods were transferred from the deep-hulled ships of the sea to flat-bottomed river boats.

The Longest River

Canada's largest river is the Mackenzie, stretching over 4 000 kilometres from its head-

Two Mackenzie Inuit hunters of the late nineteenth century. Both double-bladed and single-bladed kayak paddles were used in the Mackenzie area, and hunting weapons were lashed to the foredeck of the kayaks. Both hunters wear ivory labrets.

waters in central British Columbia to its mouth on the Arctic coast. A huge river several kilometres wide for much of its length, it has for thousands of years carried northwards rainfall from the Rocky Mountains, silt from the northern prairies and driftwood from the Liard forests. It has transported the canoes of the Indian inhabitants of the region and, for almost 200 years, those of the fur traders and many others; today the river is busy with tugs and barges plying between the railhead on Great Slave Lake and the communities and oil developments on the Beaufort Sea. Yet, because of geographical and environmental factors, the Mackenzie is one of the few great rivers of the world with no city, or even a village, at its mouth.

On the last 200 kilometres of its course, the river filters through a vast delta over 100 kilometres wide. The first European settlers, primarily interested in trapping and fur-trading, established communities in the forested southern half of the delta where Inuvik (the present administrative centre and only large town in the region) is located. The northern half of the delta, traditionally Inuit territory, is tundra, now unoccupied except for occasional oil exploration parties, summer fish camps and winter traplines. As the coastal waters in the dozens of delta channels emptying into the Beaufort Sea are too shallow

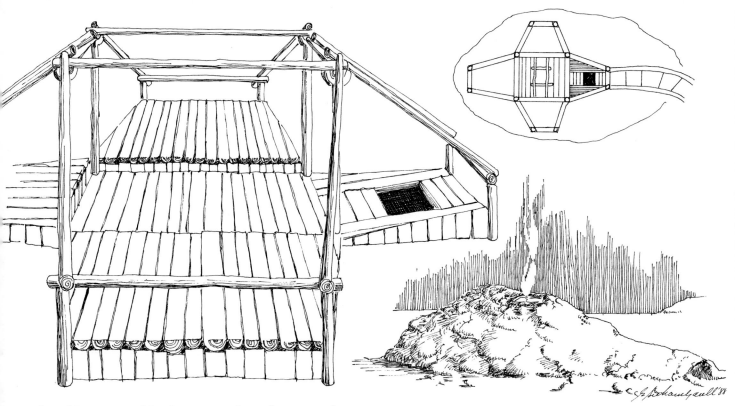

for ships, transshipping ports have been established at natural harbours such as Tuktoyaktuk to the east of the delta and Herschel Island to its west. More distant harbours are currently being dredged by the shipping and petroleum industries.

Yet long before anyone thought to search for oil in the Mackenzie Delta, before European fur-traders knew of the area, even before North America was discovered by Europeans, there was a settlement at the mouth of the Mackenzie River. Like other communities on the world's great rivers, it was a large settlement – certainly the largest occupied by the Inuit of Arctic Canada. Probably the only larger aboriginal settlements in the country were the Iroquoian agricultural communities of southern Ontario and the coastal towns of the Northwest Coast Indians. Named Kittigazuit, it was the central village of the Kittegaryumiut who, numbering 800 to 1 000, were the largest subgroup of the people later known as the Mackenzie Inuit.

A Natural Trap

Kittigazuit was built on the east bank of East Channel, the largest of the delta outlets, at the point where the channel widens into the shallow waters of Kugmallit Bay. It was located here for a very specific reason: to take advantage of geographical conditions that today prevent the area's

use as a port. Over the thousands of years that the river has flowed through this channel, the silt it carries has settled in a broad bed extending several kilometres out to sea. The silt is gradually expanding the delta seawards, and the present channel mouth is choked by small islands, some of which are revealed only at low tide. Across the eight kilometres of Kugmallit Bay there are only a few narrow channels more than two metres deep, and in many areas there are extensive shoals with water depths of only a few centimetres.

This situation forms a natural trap for the beluga, the small white whales that enter the estuary on most summer days to feed on the abundant fish in the warm river water. The operation of the trap was relatively simple, but required proper organization. When a watcher on the headland above the village reported that pods of beluga had entered the estuary, a hunt leader was hurriedly chosen and a line of kayaks slipped out of the side channel behind the village and across the estuary, downstream of the feeding whales. Up to 200 kayaks joined in such hunts and formed a line of boats at about 50-metre intervals from Kittigazuit to the opposite shore. At a signal from the leader the kayaks turned upstream, and the men shouted and smacked the water with

Artistic reconstruction of winter-festival celebrations in a house of the Kittegaryumiut. The dancer disguised as an Indian is based on Nuligak's description.

their paddles. The panicking whales fled upstream, grounding themselves on the shoals and sandbars. The oldest hunter had the privilege of throwing the first harpoon into the stranded animals, and by the time the hunt was over as many as several hundred beluga had been killed and towed to the long beach in front of the village. Although most hunts were probably much smaller, the fact that a single beluga could yield half a tonne of meat and fat indicates that the Kittegaryumiut had an extremely rich economic base on which to build their community and way of life.

Today there is little left of either the community or the way of life it represented. Modern visitors to Kittigazuit land their boats on a long gravel beach backed by a tangled windrow of driftwood logs from the upper reaches of the river. In the past these logs would have been used as fuel or as material for the construction of houses, caches, and whale-meat drying racks, tent poles, meat trays, kayak frames and dozens of other implements.

Life
in a Whaling Village

A century ago, this summer beach would have been lined with perhaps 100 or more tents and dominated by the large *kajigit*, or men's houses, where the men of the village spent most of their time when not hunting. Among the tents would have lain 100 to 200 hunting kayaks. Built for maximum speed in shallow water, these short kayaks had the upturned horns at stem and stern characteristic of Mackenzie River boats; the harpoons and lances lashed to their decks were painted with the red and black markings of individual hunters. The shoreline would have been awash with the white and red of beluga carcasses at various stages of butchering, while dark-red whale meat dried on wooden frames, and chunks of white muktuk awaited either storage in caches dug into permafrost or rendering to oil in large earthenware pots over driftwood fires. Women tended the fires; men sang and repaired their weapons in the *kajigit*, preparing themselves spiritually and physically for the next hunt; children played in the water and among the tents; and a few replete dogs slept in the sand. River ice and the high waters of autumn tides have now swept all traces of this activity from the beach in front of the settlement.

Climbing over the driftwood, the modern visitor to the site is knee-deep in lush grass and summer flowers, which feed on the approximately five hectares of the settlement's buried remains. To the north and south, slopes covered with dwarf-willow scrub rise to low plateaus dotted with the log-covered graves of the Kittegaryumiut. The only building standing on the site of the settlement – a log cabin with the doors and windows missing and the turf-covered pole-roof half collapsed – is the remains of a trading post erected in the early part of this century. Scattered over the grassy hillside, however, are a dozen or so low mounds with central depressions, the remains of aboriginal winter houses. The largest of these mounds is 10 metres long and 18 metres across; standing more than a metre higher than the surrounding surface, it represents the accumulation of several dwellings torn down and replaced over the centuries.

These houses were built of logs, in the cross-shaped pattern typical of the Mackenzie Inuit – a central floor area surrounded on three sides by alcoves containing raised sleeping platforms and on the fourth side by a sunken entrance passage. Each house was dug into the ground, and the walls and roof were heavily banked with turf insulation. Light and heat were provided by lamps burning oil rendered from beluga fat. Each structure housed up to six families, perhaps about 30 people. A century ago, six of these large houses were occupied each winter by 200 people or more. The remainder of the population wintered in smaller settlements along the river or the coast, occasionally returning to Kittigazuit to pick up sled loads of cached whale meat and oil or to celebrate the great winter solstice festivities during the dark days of December. We have only one eyewitness account of these festivities, written by Nuligak, an old man who remembered seeing them when he was six years old. As a child, he cannot have understood the spiritual significance of the events, but what he saw – the moving puppets, the stuffed bears, the dancer dressed as an Indian who entered the house with a knife and who, at the climax of his dance, disappeared amid a scatter of toys and muktuk chunks for which the children scrambled – is told in a manner that evokes the atmosphere of our own childhood memories of Christmas.

Ninety per cent of the population of Kittigazuit died from a measles epidemic in the summer of 1902. Nuligak, who was seven years old at the time, recalls that the only two men not afflicted spent the entire summer burying the dead. Even without the epidemic, the significance of Kit-

Drawing of a nineteenth-century Mackenzie Inuit chief.

broken only by the hum of mosquitoes and the paddling of swan families in the glassy water of the channel. Working during the day and walking the nearby hills at night, I became familiar with the old house mounds, the cache pits, the log graves on the plateau above the site and the scatter of artifacts to be found on the offshore silt bars at low tide. From the lookout point at the top of a high bluff I could occasionally hear the squeals of beluga in the main channel and see their white backs as they moved upstream to feed. Kittigazuit was a magical place, full of history, on those hot green days.

A week later my partner Dale Russell arrived, the weather broke, and we began work on the area of the site I had selected. Since archaeological sites even a tenth the size of Kittigazuit are usually excavated by teams ten times the size of ours, we ignored the main settlement and concentrated on a steep bank where high storm-tides were gradually eroding the remains of houses and bone middens. Cutting away the face of the wave-washed bank, we uncovered a mass of logs, artifacts and beluga bones 1.5 metres deep; the entire deposit was locked together in permanently frozen soil. Our excavations could proceed only as fast as the sun thawed this deposit, a matter of a few centimetres a day.

Along with traditional Inuit artifacts, the upper 30 centimetres contained a few European trade goods – scraps of iron and copper, fragments of china, and trade beads, including large blue beads from the Russian forts in Alaska. This portion of the deposit was obviously from the nineteenth-century occupation of the site. The second layer, almost entirely separated from the first by fragments of a log-house floor, contained similar harpoon heads and ulu blades and potsherds, but no European artifacts. We guessed that it represented occupation during the eighteenth and early nineteenth centuries. Below this was a layer of wood ash, which had probably accumulated sometime in the seventeenth century when this portion of the site was used as a dump for ashes and other refuse. This layer told us little about the site, but did serve to separate the upper layers from those below. Under the ashes we found a mass of house remains and refuse up to 60 centimetres deep, the remains of a fifteenth- and sixteenth-century occupation (as was shown later by radiocarbon dating of the material). Below this layer was the sterile clay and sand deposited by a much earlier Mackenzie River. Our small amount of archaeological work

tigazuit would probably have declined over the next few years. By this time the Kittegaryumiut had become heavily involved in the fur trade, which was so productive during those years that a successful Inuit trapper and trader could afford to have a schooner built in San Francisco and delivered to the Arctic coast. The Mackenzie Delta was rapidly filling with Nunamiut Inuit trappers from Alaska, replacing the original inhabitants who had died during the epidemics. People began to live on bacon, bannock and beans; and the beluga trap at Kittigazuit, although still used today on a small scale by hunters in motorboats, was no longer the focus of a local way of life.

I first landed at Kittigazuit on a hot and still summer day a few years ago. The weather held for the week I lived alone on the site, the silence had revealed that the whale trap and the associated village of Kittigazuit were probably used continuously for about 500 years before being abandoned early in the twentieth century.

Oral Traditions

Where did the ancestors of the beluga hunters live before settling at Kittigazuit in the fifteenth century? According to the oral tradition of the Kittegaryumiut, they and their neighbours the Kupugmiut (whose main village of Kupuk lies across East Channel from Kittigazuit) had at one time lived in two other villages some distance upstream. Shoals had formed in the channel, preventing the beluga from reaching these villages, so the people had moved downstream to the settlements occupied in the nineteenth century. Archaeological evidence confirms this story and places an approximate date on the move. One summer, while travelling by small boat down East Channel, I visited two old village sites facing each other across the river, approximately 10 kilometres upstream from Kittigazuit and Kupuk. Although today the river downstream from the sites is too shallow to allow beluga to reach the area, beluga bones protruded from the eroded banks in front of each village. Among the bones were artifacts similar to those from the lowest levels of the Kittigazuit dig. Two radiocarbon dates suggest that the old villages were occupied during the fourteenth or fifteenth century. It seems likely, therefore, that local oral tradition has not only preserved the memories of these villages for approximately 500 years, but has also helped to reveal why they were abandoned and the village of Kittigazuit was consequently founded.

The ancient heritage of the Kittegaryumiut is not likely to be preserved for many more years. Not only are the oral traditions dying with the old people, but most of the archaeological sites in the area are rapidly disappearing because of coastal erosion. Nuvurak, which was a large, thriving village in 1826 when Sir John Richardson passed by, has now vanished and is marked only by a few stone tools scattered over the outer beach at low tide. Other sites are threatened by bulldozers building airstrips, harbours and roads for the petroleum industry. Kittigazuit itself is slowly crumbling into the river. Without archaeological attention in the near future, most of the evidence of this unique settlement and way of life will be lost forever.

CHAPTER 16

A REMARKABLE PAST

All genuine archaeological evidence confirms that the ancestors of Canada's native peoples developed unique cultures independently of the influence of any imaginary early immigrants from Europe or other worlds. The outstanding accomplishments of those cultures deserve our proud recognition.

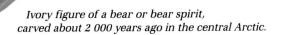

*Ivory figure of a bear or bear spirit,
carved about 2 000 years ago in the central Arctic.*

North American prehistory is a standard subject of the tabloid press, often receiving the kind of exploitive coverage given to flying saucers, the Bermuda Triangle, miracle cures for obesity, and the unlikely romantic entanglements of entertainers. Interestingly enough, articles on North America's distant past in the tabloids rarely mention native Indians. Rather, the major actors seem to be Vikings, Phoenicians, Irishmen, Egyptians, Welshmen, the Lost Tribes of Israel, and many other Old World peoples who purportedly visited or occupied our continent at various times in the distant past.

The view of the New World as a host continent to ancient visitors from abroad is deeply rooted. It began with speculation on the origins of the New World Indians. In 1537, 45 years after Columbus's first voyage, Pope Paul III issued a bull proclaiming that the Indians were human, a fact that had been disputed by some early Spanish settlers. Being human, they were therefore considered descendants of Adam and Eve and, more immediately, the family of Noah. Yet Noah's three sons were said to have settled the three continents of the Old World – Europe, Asia and Africa. In the framework of biblical interpretation, the Indians were a distinct problem. One early solution, first proposed in the sixteenth century and still occasionally advanced, traced the aboriginal peoples to the ten tribes of Israel who disappeared into Assyrian bondage during the eighth century B.C. and are never mentioned again in the Bible. A variant of this theory is a basic tenet of the Mormon church: the Book of Mormon, which appeared in the early nineteenth century, tells of an Israelite prophet named Lehi who, receiving divine warning of an Assyrian attack, led his people by boat from the Red Sea to the west coast of South America, where they became the ancestors of the first American Indians.

The Heirs of Atlantis

Another early explanation of Indian origins was the story of the lost continent of Atlantis, mentioned by Plato and embellished by many later authors on the basis of various, usually mystical, evidence. Atlantis was gradually transformed by the mystics into a fabulous continent inhabited by remarkably rich and cultivated people; when the continent sank beneath the waves of the Atlantic at some time in the past, its population fled to the New World, where it began a long process of cultural degeneration. With its legendary companion continent Lemuria, a Pacific version of Atlantis first described in the nineteenth century, Atlantis is still occasionally advanced as the place of Indian origins.

A more sensible and prosaic theory was put forward as early as 1590 by the learned Fray José de Acosta. He postulated that the first Indians were small groups of Asiatic hunters who had wandered slowly eastwards to North America, either entirely or mainly by land. Almost 400 years later, our much broader geographical knowledge of the regions between Asia and America can add nothing to Acosta's theory, but only confirm its accuracy. We can also be fairly certain that in the sixteenth century Acosta's ideas on prehistory attracted little popular attention.

A Hint of Racism

Most tabloid prehistory is characterized by a covert racism, exploiting a belief that only Europeans could have introduced the elements of civilization undeniably present in the New World prior to the time of Columbus. This is nowhere more apparent than in the theory of the Mound Builders, which was introduced in eighteenth-century America and not discredited until the present century. As European settlers pressed westwards over the mountains of eastern North America and into the fertile farmlands of the Mississippi and Ohio valleys, they found these regions inhabited by the displaced vestiges of earlier Indian nations, decimated by centuries of exposure to European disease and native trade wars. They also found the remains of man-made structures – huge earthen mounds shaped like animals or pyramids or temple mounds. Excavation of these mounds revealed elaborately decorated pottery and beautiful objects fashioned of polished stone, shell, copper and other materials – obviously the remains of a sophisticated population.

People of the time found it difficult to believe what we now know to be true – that these mounds were built by the ancestors of the local Indians. Instead, they postulated an earlier race of Mound Builders who had inhabited the continent until they were driven away by the Indians, leaving behind only their architectural monuments. The creation of this imaginary race of Mound Builders spawned many fanciful notions among nineteenth-century writers. In the words of Robert Silverberg, author of a recent book on the Mound Builders myth: "The dream of a lost prehistoric race in the American heartland was profoundly satisfying; and if the vanished ones had been giants, or white men, or Israelites, or Danes, or Toltecs, or great white Jewish Toltec Vikings, so much the better." Erich von Daniken, a German writer who explains most ancient monuments in North America (and elsewhere in the world) as the works of visitors from space, only pushes the Mound Builder myth to its extreme.

Although the great earthen constructions of the North American Midwest are now rarely disputed as the work of Indians, there are persistent claims that the continent was visited or inhabited in prehistoric times by various Old World peoples. The most outrageous recent theories are those of Barry Fell, a retired marine biologist and amateur epigraphist who has written two books on the subject. Not content, as are most of his rivals, with crediting the Romans or the Egyptians or the Vikings or the Irish with early voyages to America, Fell backs all of the above and several other groups besides.

In his scattergun theorizing on how prehistoric America was populated, Fell makes the following suggestions, among others: Bronze Age Scandinavians in southern Ontario; Carthaginian traders importing manufactured goods in exchange for furs and gold during the first millennium B.C.; early Celtic settlers in New England; Jewish refugees from Roman oppression fleeing to Kentucky; Libyan Christians fleeing the Vandals and settling in western North America about A.D. 500, followed shortly by various Moslem and Byzantine groups; and the Vikings exploring and settling most of the continent.

Spurious Evidence

The evidence used by Fell and his supporters is as varied as are the purported ancient voyagers. Most common are "inscriptions" on rocks, which Fell seemingly finds everywhere and which he claims are in a variety of ancient alphabets and languages. A self-taught epigraphist, Fell appears to have remarkable success in deciphering "inscriptions" that geologists identify as natural weathering patterns on rocks or marks made on fieldstones by farmers' ploughs and harrows. Professional epigraphists do not support his decipherings; they discredit his Egyptian hieroglyphs and describe his Norse runes and Celtic ogham as either modern fakes or mere random scratches. Unfortunately for Fell's theory, the inscriptions that he claims are in the ancient Celto-Iberian language have been claimed by other amateur epigraphists to be in Phoenician or in the language of the Minoan civilization. Fell has even been known to claim that the same inscription belonged to two unrelated ancient languages.

One of the most impressive inscriptions used by Fell to support his views is the Davenport Stone, a circular piece of slate inscribed with unusual alphabet-like markings, which was excavated from an Indian burial mound in Iowa during the late nineteenth century. This object has long been recognized as a fake, planted where it would be found by an enthusiastic but unpopular local preacher who was also an amateur archaeologist. The stone bearing the carved inscription came from the wall of the Old Slate House, a local brothel, and there are published statements by people who admitted to participating in the prank. But Fell ignores this evidence and continues to treat the Davenport Stone as the Rosetta Stone of the New World.

The other evidence produced by Fell and his supporters is as insubstantial as the "inscriptions" are. In New England, the ruins of "stone temples" supposedly built by prehistoric Celtic peoples have been proved by both archaeologists and historians to be root cellars and other structures built by Colonial farmers. The attribution of some place-names in eastern North America to Celtic origins has been shown by linguists to be equally unfounded, as are the linguistic relationships between Algonquian languages and various Old World languages. Yet, although he presents no shred of reliable evidence to support the theory of early transatlantic voyages, Fell's books continue to sell to a North American public apparently intent on believing that their own Old World ancestors had an ancient heritage on this continent.

Mythical Vikings

Probably the most popular of the mythical voyagers to North America are the Vikings. Medieval Norse seamen, working their way westwards through the islands of the North Atlantic, reached Iceland by about A.D. 860 and Greenland by about A.D. 980. Within a few decades they made tentative explorations farther west, where they discovered, and briefly attempted to settle, a country known as Vinland. Out of these few

continued page 168

HUMAN HISTORY

YEARS AGO	AFRICA	EURASIA	NEW WORLD
500	European exploration and colonization		Aztec Empire
1 000			
2 000		Roman Empire	Cities, writing
5 000	Egyptian pyramids, writing	Cities, writing	
7 500			Agriculture
10 000	Agriculture	Agriculture	
15 000			First occupation
25 000		Cave paintings	
50 000		First burials	
100 000			
200 000			
500 000		Standardized stone tools First use of fire	
1 000 000	First stone tools		
4 000 000	First ancestors with upright posture		
10 000 000	Larger primates, ancestral to apes and humans, appear in Africa and Asia		
60 000 000	Small primates, ancestral to monkeys, apes and humans appear after age of the dinosaurs		

Pre-human ancestors

Homo erectus

Homo sapiens

CANADIAN PREHISTORY

YEARS AGO	ARCTIC	WEST COAST	PRAIRIES	EASTERN WOODLANDS	ATLANTIC
100	KITTIGAZUIT	KITWANGA	Horses introduced		
500	Little Ice Age			HOCHELAGA Huronia	European exploration
1 000	Thule Inuit migration		WRITING-ON-STONE	PETER-BOROUGH PETROGLYPHS	
2 000	Dorset Culture		OLD WOMEN'S BUFFALO JUMP	SERPENT MOUND	Burial mounds
3 000	Palaeo-Eskimo occupation				
5 000		First shell middens			
7 500			First buffalo jumps		L'ANSE-AMOUR
10 000					Early maritime hunters
15 000 ±	BLUEFISH CAVES				

Palaeolithic big-game hunters

Indian hunters

Indian farmers

Paleo-Eskimo hunters

Inuit hunters

Sites mentioned in the book are printed in capital letters.

historical facts has grown an entire mythology about the voyages and land takings, which has placed Viking settlements as far west as Oregon and as far south as Paraguay.

The evidence for such settlement is very similar to that presented as proof of earlier voyagers: faked or misinterpreted "inscriptions", misidentified artifacts, and ruins of stone buildings. An old stone tower in Newport, Rhode Island, built as a windmill during the Colonial period (as shown by historical records and archaeological excavation), has been misinterpreted by Fell and others as the remains of a Norse cathedral. A stone found near Kensington, Minnesota, in the late nineteenth century is carved with a runic message telling of a Norse expedition to the area. Although immediately recognized and denounced as a forgery, the Kensington stone has led to a flood of spurious evidence in support of a Norse occupation of this area: nineteenth-century tobacco cutters are identified as Norse battle-axes; blasting holes drilled in rocks by farmers clearing their fields are identified as "mooring holes" designed to anchor Viking ships (although the Norse never used mooring holes in the Old World). A cache of genuine Norse weapons, purportedly found in the northwestern Ontario bush in 1926 but quickly proved to be twentieth-century imports from Norway, is still touted as evidence of ancient Norse visitors. Stone houses and cairns built by the Palaeo-Eskimos of northern Quebec are misinterpreted as the remains of Norse villages. There appears to be no end to the spurious finds and arguments constantly emerging in support of prehistoric Viking settlement in the New World.

Rather surprisingly, the one site generally accepted by archaeologists as proof of Norse visitors – L'Anse aux Meadows, at the northern tip of Newfoundland – is almost universally rejected as a fake by those who persist in believing that North America once supported a thriving Norse population. Perhaps this is because archaeology only confirms what the Norse sagas and common sense tell us – that the Greenlandic Norse did discover this continent but probably made only a few tentative attempts at colonization on the northeastern coast of Canada, the region closest and most similar to their North Atlantic homeland.

What lesson is there in this sorry tale of muddle and misunderstanding? For one thing, we are made aware of the deep public interest in our prehistoric past – that longing for heritage mentioned at the beginning of this book. More importantly, we learn that the view of Canadian prehistory held by most archaeologists working in the country has not been adequately presented to the public. The myths of an ancient Canada occupied by Romans or Vikings or spacemen have had little competition in the media and have generally gone unchallenged, perhaps because archaeologists feel their information is not as "interesting" as the tabloid prehistory of Barry Fell, Erich von Daniken and their associates. Archaeologists must more vigorously present their own views of Canada's prehistory and more forcefully reject the unsubstantiated claims of fanciful popularizers of history.

The ancient Egyptians, Chinese, Phoenicians and Romans had very little to do with the Canadian past. The Norse were here, and small groups may have made a brief attempt to colonize areas along the east coast, but they left no lasting mark on the continent. The ancestors of native Canadians who immigrated from Siberia over 10 000 years ago, however, did some remarkable things. They hunted elephants in southern Canada along the margins of the retreating Ice Age glacier. They built the burial mound at L'Anse-Amour 7 000 years ago, at a time when the ancestors of most Europeans were hunting deer and boar in the forest wilderness. Later, some imported trade goods and religious ideas that had originated in the great civilizations of Central America, while others developed innovative ways of life that made possible the occupation of territory as barren as the High Arctic islands.

All genuine archaeological evidence confirms that the ancestors of the native Canadians developed unique cultures independently of the influence of any imaginary early immigrants from Europe or other worlds. The outstanding accomplishments of those cultures deserve our proud recognition.

ACKNOWLEDGEMENTS

This book owes much to my colleagues in the study of Canadian archaeology. The following individuals patiently checked the accuracy of the chapters that deal with their work, or were generous in providing ideas and illustrations: Jack Brink, Jacques Cinq-Mars, Jerome Cybulski, William Finlayson, Hugh Dempsey, Richard Forbis, the late Richard Johnston, George MacDonald, Peter Storck, Patricia Sutherland, Bruce Trigger, James Tuck, William Workman, James Wright. Most of the chapters were previously published in Canadian Heritage magazine, and I thank the Heritage Canada Foundation for agreeing to their republication in this book. My greatest debt is to Patricia Sutherland, whose help and encouragement over the years have been invaluable.

ROBERT McGHEE, the author, was born in Wiarton, Ontario, and received his training in archaeology at the University of Toronto and the University of Calgary. Since 1965 he has done fieldwork in Arctic Canada from Labrador to the Mackenzie Delta; it has been primarily concerned with tracing the history of the Canadian Inuit and the development of their unique way of life. He has published many books and articles on Canadian archaeology. Dr. McGhee is currently head of the Scientific Section, Archaeological Survey of Canada, Canadian Museum of Civilization.

GILLES ARCHAMBAULT, the painter, has created thirty-one original works for *Ancient Canada*. He turned from photography to painting during the 1970s, and has become well known both as a painter and book illustrator. His works have been exhibited in Montréal, Ottawa, Toronto and Boston, and he is represented in collections in Canada, the United States, France and Saudi Arabia.

HARRY FOSTER, the photographer, was born in Montréal. He has worked in both Canada and New Zealand, and is currently chief photographer, Canadian Museum of Civilization. His photographs play an important part in all the Museum's major books and exhibition catalogues.

INDEX

Printed in Canada